# COMFORT
## *VERSUS*
# BUSINESS

## WHAT WOULD IT COST TO
## <u>KEEP</u> GOING?

ALUEL D. DENG

Publisher: Independent Publishing Network.
Publication Date: 9th January 2024
ISBN: 978-1-80517-353-3
Author: Aluel D. Deng

Readers, the time is now.
Embrace change.
New is scary, but new is also profitable.

# SELF

Flesh. Body. Mind. Soul.

At the surface level, it may seem like the pursuit of self-awareness is a selfish endeavour. After all, self-awareness can often involve a deep introspection and focus on one's own desires and needs; but upon closer examination, it becomes evident that self-awareness is not about selfishness, but rather about understanding and embracing the true essence of oneself.

To truly gain control over oneself, it is important to live in true authenticity. This means embracing strengths and weaknesses, desires and fears, and not being afraid to be vulnerable and open. Authenticity requires us to confront the various aspects of ourselves, both positive and negative, and to accept them as a whole.

Living in authenticity also requires us to let go of the fear of the unknown. Often, we are hesitant to step out of our comfort zones and take risks because we are afraid of what might happen.

We fear failure, rejection, and judgment. However, it is through pushing our boundaries and embracing -

uncertainty that we can truly grow and evolve as individuals. It is in moments of adversity that we truly discover who we are and what we are capable of.

Controlling our minds in a world where so much is out of our control can be a daunting task. Our thoughts are often influenced by external factors such as societal expectations, peer pressure, and cultural norms. It is easy to lose ourselves in the noise of the world and live according to the expectations of others. It's important to note that true self-control comes from being able to detach ourselves from these external influences and to listen to our inner voice.

In the battle between reality and morality, we often find ourselves heavily conflicted between what we want to do and what we should do. It is in these moments that our self-awareness is truly tested. The epitome of a self-aware person seeks reward faster than the ordinary being, but they also understand the importance of aligning their desires with their values. This requires a deep understanding of oneself and a commitment to living in accordance with one's own principles - something I haven't yet mastered.

You see in everything we do, there is a small window of decision making, whether moral or immoral, rational or irrational, honest or dishonest; you are in full control of what happens next based on a decision that you made seconds before. A decision that can either bring you moments of pure pleasure or extreme restlessness.

There are often factors that haunt our thoughts, not with mere ponderings but inquiries into the essence of our -

existence. They delve into the realms of flesh, body, mind and soul, unravelling the intricate tapestry that forms our true self.

The flesh, our physical being, is the vessel through which we experience the world. It encompasses our senses, allowing us to touch, taste, smell, see, and hear the beauty and chaos that surrounds us. It is through the flesh that we dance, embrace, and feel the warmth of a loved one's touch. Yet, it can also be a source of vulnerability and limitation. Society often sets standards and expectations for the flesh, condemning imperfections and emphasizing beauty. It is in these moments that we must transcend societal constraints and embrace our unique physicality, recognizing that beauty lies not only in the eye of the beholder but within our own self-perception.

The body, while closely intertwined with the flesh, extends beyond its physicality. It encompasses our thoughts, emotions, and actions. It is the realm of the mind, where ideas take shape and dreams are born. The body possesses immense potential, but it can also be a battleground between our desires and our conscience. It is here that the struggle between what we want to do and what we should do emerges. It is in this internal conflict that the true nature of our character is revealed. To gain mastery over the body, we must navigate the labyrinth of decision-making. We must choose virtues over vices, integrity over dishonesty, and rationality over impulsiveness. This constant battle of self-control shapes our destiny and moulds us into the person we aspire to be.

However, the soul, a deep reflection from the mind, the most intangible and enigmatic aspect of our being, is the true essence of who we are.

It transcends mortal boundaries and connects us to something greater than ourselves. It is where compassion, love, and spirituality reside. The soul is the seat of our deepest emotions and our most profound experiences. To know oneself at the deepest level is to delve into the recesses of the soul, to listen to its whispers and honour its yearnings. It is here that we find our purpose, our passion, and our connection to the world around us. Acknowledging the significance of the soul is the key to unlocking our full potential.

To traverse the realms of flesh, body, mind and soul, one must embark on a journey of self-discovery and self-acceptance. We must shed the shackles of fear and embrace chaos as a catalyst for growth. It is only in authentic living that we can truly harness the power of self-control and become the architect of our destiny.

By embracing our physicality, mastering our thoughts and actions, and tapping into the depths of our soul, we unlock our true potential. It is through this profound understanding of self that we can navigate the complexities of life and become the person we envision ourselves to be. So, let us embrace the challenge of answering the question, *'Who am I, and who do I want to be?'*, and in doing so, embark on a transformative journey of self-discovery.

*\*\*\**

The year was 2016, and the cold winter wind howled outside my bedroom window, casting a gloomy shadow over the London skyline. After a tiring day at college, I found myself lying on my bed, contemplating my future.

Deep within me, I knew that I was destined for something greater, that I possessed a restless creativity that yearned to be unleashed. However, I was plagued by the uncertainty of how to channel this drive into practicality.

As I lay there, lost in thought, the low murmur of the television in front of me distracted my attention. An advertisement about crowdfunding played in the background, initially nothing more than noise. Yet, something about it caught my attention, urging me to delve deeper and explore what this concept truly entailed. Intrigued by this unfamiliar term, I decided to conduct some research to understand the world of investment and the opportunities it held.

Being an amateur in the realm of anything business related, that seemingly inconspicuous moment marked a turning point in my life. It ignited a spark of curiosity within me, a desire to explore and understand the labyrinthine world of investment and entrepreneurship. Little did I know at the time, but that gloomy winter evening became the catalyst that fuelled my innate craving for more, propelling me onto a path of discovery and growth.

Venturing into investment research, more particularly, crowdfunding, I realized it was far more than just a financial tool. It was a revolution that democratized access to capital, paving the way for aspiring entrepreneurs and visionaries who lacked conventional means of funding. No longer bound by traditional gatekeepers, individuals from all walks of life could seek support for their innovative ideas, bringing them to life with the backing of a community of believers.

With each click and scroll, my understanding of crowdfunding deepened, revealing the vast number of success stories it had facilitated. Entrepreneurs who had once been confined to the outskirts of the business world were now flourishing, armed with the support of their backers and investors. The stories of triumph and resilience inspired me, kindling a burning desire within me to pursue my own entrepreneurial dreams.

The more I delved into the world of capital investment, the more I realized that crowdfunding had its potential as a platform for creative expression and social change. It wasn't merely about raising funds; it was about uniting people who shared a common vision, who believed in the power of ideas to shape the world. It was about empowering the individual, providing a platform to transform dreams into reality, and challenging the status quo.

Emboldened by my newfound knowledge and motivated by the stories of crowdfunding success, I began to envision my own potential. I recognized that the spark of creativity within me had the power to ignite change and make a meaningful impact. It was no longer a restless yearning without direction; instead, it had transformed into a driving force propelling me towards the pursuit of entrepreneurial endeavours.

From that pivotal winter evening in 2016, my life took on a renewed sense of purpose. I immersed myself in learning about business strategies, marketing techniques, and entrepreneurial best practices. Armed with my research and driven by the passion ignited within me, I started to shape my dreams into tangible goals.

As I sit here, reflecting upon that gloomy, Winter evening, I am grateful for the path it set me on. It served as motivation for my personal and professional growth, instilling a deep-rooted determination to never settle for mediocrity. The world of entrepreneurship opened my eyes to the endless possibilities that lay ahead and inspiredme to embrace the restless creativity within me.

*\*\*\**

Frantically searching the web well into the early hours of the morning, there was a profound silence in my bedroom, just the soft tapping of my laptop's keyboard, coupled with eery nothingness.

Naively, a search tab was open, 'how do people get investment', shortly another tab opened, 'what type of businesses are doing well in 2016'. I went into a deep rabbit hole of attempting to gain sufficient knowledge to armour me in a 'dog eat dog' world of entrepreneurship.

Unsatisfied with just knowing the current market trends, I clicked and searched on the final tab, 'e-commerce business stats in 2016.' This search in particular, further deepened my understanding of the digital landscape. Rapid technological advancements and the expanding online consumer base made e-commerce an appealing avenue for entrepreneurial endeavours.
I discovered the importance of engaging user experiences, effective digital marketing strategies, and the vital role of data analytics in e-commerce success. The potential to reach a global audience from the comfort of my own home was incredibly enticing.

Armed with this wealth of knowledge, my mind buzzed with ideas for my first business venture.

The thought of creating something from scratch, implementing the newly acquired skills, and impacting people's lives excited me beyond measure. It propelled me to meticulously plan every aspect of my business, from identifying my target audience to establishing a unique value proposition.

As I immersed myself in this planning phase, doubts inevitably crept in. Would my business succeed? Do I have what it takes to compete in the cutthroat business world? However, I fiercely believed that failure was not an option. The pressure I felt to prove myself, not to others, but to myself, became a driving force. I was determined to overcome any obstacle, learn from every setback, and persevere until success was attained.

Looking back, that unplanned journey into the depths of the internet served as a catalyst for my entrepreneurial aspirations. It awakened within me a sense of purpose, a burning desire to manifest the potential that lay dormant. I now understood that capability and success were not elusive concepts reserved for the select few, but rather attainable through perseverance, continuous self-improvement, and unwavering determination.

Though my first business venture may have been destined to go either way, success or failure, it was the first step in my journey towards fulfilling my dreams.

# DISCOVERY

It is a daunting decision to deviate from the path that society expects us to follow. From a young age, we are bombarded with societal norms and expectations. We are taught that success is measured by material possessions, status, and a secure job. Our dreams and aspirations are often pushed aside in favour of the practical and safe choices.

But for those who have made the decision to follow their true calling, they understand that life is not just about reaching the destination, but about the journey itself. It is about finding fulfilment, purpose, and happiness in what they do. They understand that pursuing their true passion may not guarantee immediate success or financial stability, but it brings them a sense of inner satisfaction that cannot be found elsewhere.

These individuals have endured countless moments of doubt, fear, and uncertainty. They have faced societal judgment and criticism for their unconventional choices. They have experienced setbacks and failures along the way. Yet, despite all of this, they remain steadfast in their decision.

They understand that the road less travelled may be difficult, but it is worth it. They have seen too many individuals follow the conventional route only to end up feeling unfulfilled and regretful. They refuse to settle for a life that is not aligned with their true purpose.

These brave souls have taken risks, made sacrifices, and put in the hard work necessary to succeed in their chosen path. They have learned to trust their instincts and intuition, even when the world around them tells them otherwise. They have found the courage to pursue their dreams, no matter how uncertain or unconventional they may be.

The reward for their decision is not always immediate, but it is profound. They experience a sense of fulfilment and joy that goes beyond material possessions or external recognition. They wake up each day excited to pursue their passions and make a difference in the world. Their work becomes their purpose, and their purpose becomes their life.

If life were truly a game, these individuals would be the ones who have achieved the highest level of success. Not because they have accumulated the most wealth or achieved the highest status, but because they have followed their true calling and lived a life that aligns with their deepest desires.

So, if you ever find yourself at a crossroads in life, faced with the message, 'It's time to make a decision on the route you would like to take', remember the power of following your true calling. Choose the path that sets your soul on fire, even if it may deviate from what is expected. Embrace the silent battle within yourself and have the courage to pursue your dreams.

In the end, it is not about the destination, but about the journey and the desire that comes from living a life true to oneself.

*\*\*\**

Nearing the end of 2016, the hair and the beauty industry was booming. Everyone wanted to know the secrets behind celebrity hair, and one of those secrets was raw, unprocessed hair extensions. Recognizing this trend, I quickly saw an opportunity to capitalize on the demand for high-quality hair products. I knew that in order to succeed, I needed to understand the industry inside and out.

There was a plethora of questions that plagued my mind as I fought through the challenges of starting my own business. As I continued to research and immerse myself in the market, I realized that I had the potential to be more than just a novice. I had the drive and determination to become a skilled entrepreneur.

My journey began and ended with late nights filled with diagrams, bullet points, and presentations. I was determined to learn everything there was to know about the hair and makeup market. It wasn't always easy. I sacrificed sleep and relied heavily on coffee to keep me going. My hands grew stiff from typing, but I pushed through, fuelled by my passion for the trade.

Through my extensive research, I gained knowledge that set me apart from others. I didn't just rely on search engines for information; I went a step further and sought out trade secrets from successful entrepreneurs. This knowledge gave me a competitive edge and allowed me to navigate the industry with confidence.

I understood that trends change, and in order to succeed as an entrepreneur, I needed to stay ahead of the curve. By choosing a niche within the beauty industry that I, as a woman, could relate to, I positioned myself to cater to the needs and desires of my target audience. This understanding gave me the upper hand in maximizing sales.

As days turned into weeks, and weeks into months, I dedicated each day to building the framework of my business plan. Every evening was spent exploring the market, understanding customer preferences, and fine-tuning my strategies. It was an arduous process, but I knew that the hard work would pay off.

One particular hurdle I faced was communication with international hair vendors. The language barrier and pricing challenges often left me frustrated. As an amateur, I struggled with negotiation and lacked the confidence to navigate these obstacles. There were moments when quitting seemed appealing, when the fear of failure seemed overwhelming. But I recognized that these doubts were simply imposter syndrome, a temporary roadblock on my journey to success.

I reminded myself of the potential I possessed and realized that the doubt and uncertainty I was feeling stemmed from the fear of venturing into the unknown. But I also knew that in order to grow and achieve my goals, I needed to push past this fear and embrace the possibilities that lay ahead.

# CONTROL

Emotions play a significant role in our decision-making process, often clouding our judgment and disassociating us from harsh realities. This truth becomes apparent when we reflect upon the potential consequences of our past decisions. What if we had chosen differently ten years ago? Where would we find ourselves at this very moment? What if we had suppressed our frustration last week? Would it have altered the course of events?

The path we choose at any stage of our lives requires a certain level of discipline, enabling us to make decisions that align with our goals and aspirations. However, this pursuit of direction is often hindered by distractions and external influences. For instance, adhering to a strict routine often invites intrusive thoughts and temptations, making it arduous to follow through with resolutions or plans. The brain, wired to resist constraints and labels, often generates an inclination to do the opposite of what is required. This internal reverse psychology can be as deceiving as the external factors affecting our decision-making.

Imagine you made a critical decision ten years ago that led you down a different path.

Perhaps you pursued a different career or decided to move to a new city. The consequences of that choice would have undoubtedly shaped your present reality. The people you would have met, the experiences you would have had, and the opportunities that might have arisen are all variables that could have altered your life's trajectory. It is fascinating to think about the multitude of possibilities that might have unfolded had you have chosen differently.

Similarly, suppressing frustration or any negative emotion in the past can have a profound impact on subsequent events. We all encounter moments of frustration, where the natural inclination is to react impulsively; but if we manage to restrain ourselves and handle the situation with grace and composure, the outcome might be entirely different. Suppressing frustration can prevent us from making rash decisions or engaging in regrettable actions that may have long-lasting consequences. By maintaining control over our emotions, we have the power to shape the outcomes of our daily experiences.

The interplay between emotions, decision-making, and reality is undeniably complex. It is crucial to acknowledge the role emotions play in our lives and be aware of their influence on our decision-making processes. With that being said, discipline and self-control can break the cycle of emotional dissociation from reality. By developing a greater understanding of our emotions and actively managing them, we can make more informed decisions and navigate the complexities of life with clarity. A lack of emotive control is bound to have a profound impact on the decisions we make and can often disassociate us from the reality unfolding around us.

Contemplating the potential consequences of alternate choices in the past allows us to recognize the power our -

decisions hold. Suppressing negative emotions can alter the trajectory of events and potentially bring about different outcomes. By acknowledging the influence of emotions and cultivating discipline, we can strive for a more conscious and purposeful approach to decision-making, bridging the gap between our emotions and the reality we all must face.

***

As I embarked on my first entrepreneurial journey, Luxy Lox, a hair extension business, faced numerous challenges and doubts. The fear of failure within me was constantly hovering, reminding me of the potential risks and unknowns that lay ahead. However, I refused to succumb to the pessimistic thoughts and instead decided to shift my focus towards strategic thinking and a positive mindset.

By redirecting my thoughts towards strategic planning, I was able to envision the path I needed to take in order to establish successful partnerships and expand the customer base. The initial international calls that seemed daunting at first were transformed into valuable collaborations.

With strategic thinking as my guiding principle, the sleepless nights gradually lessened, making way for a healthier routine that prioritized optimal performance. I realized that being well-rested and mentally sharp was crucial in order to make sound decisions and effectively manage the day-to-day operations of the business.

In order to transform Luxy Lox from a mere business plan into a tangible reality, I harnessed my strategic thinking skills to develop an engaging and user-friendly website.

This online platform became a main channel for displaying the products, attracting potential customers, and ultimately converting leads into sales. I was committed to providing visitors with an immersive and personalized experience, ensuring that every aspect of the website catered to their needs.

Converting leads was not an easy task, as it required dedicated effort and attention to detail. But I was determined to go the extra mile for every customer. I spent countless hours interacting with them, addressing their queries, and ensuring that their specific needs were met. It was an exhausting endeavour, especially as I was still schooling and often had mountains of coursework to attend to, but the reward of seeing a satisfied customer and the positive reviews that followed fuelled my passion and reaffirmed my belief in the success of Luxy Lox.

As time went on, I started to realize that I couldn't do it all by myself. My workload was becoming overwhelming, and I knew that if I wanted to take my new creation to the next level, I needed help. So, I took a leap of faith and accepted a friend's offer to help me sustain the business.

At first, it was difficult to let go of some of the control. I had been so used to doing everything myself that it was hard to trust someone else to do it as well as I could. But I quickly learned that I couldn't grow if I didn't delegate. My friend turned out to be a valuable asset to not only me, but in helping to lay the foundations of the business, taking on tasks that I simply didn't have the expertise for.

With the help of my friend, Luxy Lox began to thrive. I took the opportunity to innocently improve the website, as well as implement new marketing strategies, solely focusing on popular social media platforms.

But fruition didn't come without its challenges. As Luxy Lox grew, so did the competition. More companies entered the market, offering similar products at lower prices, with more experienced entrepreneurs and heavier pockets. I knew that if I wanted to stay ahead, I had to innovate and differentiate myself from the competition.

The day began like any other. I woke up, got ready, and headed off to college, my routine carefully followed. Classes came and went, filled with lectures, discussions, and assignments. But my mind was no longer solely focused on textbooks and academic pursuits. It was consumed by the ambition that had taken root in my heart, the burning desire to build something of my own; which I, out of curiosity, attempted.

As the founder and sole proprietor, Luxy Lox demanded my undivided attention. I juggled between attending classes, rushing home to fulfil orders, and managing most aspects of the business, despite the helping hand. It was challenging, but I was fuelled by a sense of purpose. I believed in my products and the impact they could have on others.

Every inquiry received through the live chat system sparked curiosity and a desire to assist. The interactions were not just robotic exchanges of information; they were genuine conversations that brought a personal touch to the online shopping experience. Each conversation presented a new challenge, a unique opportunity to provide tailored solutions and exceed customer expectations. Being able to effectively guide customers and address their concerns instilled a sense of gratification knowing that I was contributing to their satisfaction.

Observing their needs, providing advice, and ultimately witnessing them satisfied, not only reinforced their trust in the new business, but also encapsulated the essence of the role I played. From the initial greeting to the final "thank you for your purchase," each step represented a personal touch, uniquely crafted to bring joy and satisfaction to the customer.

And then, suddenly, it all stopped. I still remember the day when the messages ceased to appear, the chat system remaining silent and lifeless. The anxiety that once propelled me to work harder turned into confusion and worry. What had gone wrong? Did I lose my touch? Were my products no longer in demand? These questions haunted me, dimming the once bright light that illuminated my path.

Days turned into weeks, and the silence persisted. The absence of customer interactions allowed doubts to seep into my mind. I questioned the viability of my business, fearing that it was all just a fleeting dream. But as the turmoil settled within me, a sense of resilience emerged.

# OVERINDULGENCE

Whether it is our consumption of indulgent treats or our choices regarding our personal focus points, striking a balance is crucial. Too often, we become enthralled by a pursuit without considering the consequences that may manifest over time.

The example of devouring chocolate bars may seem trivial initially, but it serves as a metaphor for our tendency to become consumed by our desires. It starts innocently enough - one chocolate bar that brings immense pleasure. The taste is so delightful, it tempts us to consume another, and then another. Before we realize it, minutes turn into days, and the occasional indulgence transforms into a daily routine. This process of habituation is insidious, gradually taking hold of our lives until it becomes difficult to resist.

Eventually, guilt creeps in, overshadowing any initial longing. We recognize the detrimental impact our actions have had on our well-being. We might attempt desperate measures to rectify the damage - extreme fasting or increased water intake - but the damage is already done. Our pores become clogged, our teeth riddled with cavities, and the threat of diabetes looms ominously on the horizon.

This is a cautionary tale, as it highlights the dangers of excess. Our inability to exercise discernment and moderation can lead us down a treacherous path. It raises questions about our inherent optimism or perhaps our sheer ignorance. Are we blindly entering situations, hoping for the best, or are we simply being foolish?

The parallels between this example and our personal focus points are striking. We often throw ourselves wholeheartedly into endeavours without truly considering the consequences. Ambition can be a double-edged sword - a powerful motivator, yet also a source of destruction. When our ambitions are not balanced by a careful consideration of the potential impact on our well-being, relationships, and overall happiness, we risk falling into a cycle of chasing success at all costs.

There is indeed a fine line between ambition and destruction, one that we continually navigate in our lives. It takes self-awareness, reflection, and a willingness to reassess our priorities to maintain equilibrium.

Just as we need to monitor our consumption of chocolate bars, we must evaluate our passions and aspirations to determine if they are leading us closer to fulfilment or bordering on self-destruction. It is essential to find that delicate balance between ambition and self-care.

This involves considering the potential long-term consequences, finding time for self-reflection, and seeking support from loved ones to keep us accountable. By cultivating a sense of discernment and self-awareness, we can avoid the pitfalls of excessive ambition and ensure healthier, more sustainable paths to success.

Our tendency to indulge without restraint extends beyond just our preferences for chocolate bars. It symbolizes our inclination to become consumed by desires, pursuits, and ambition. It is crucial to recognize the potential harm in excess and strive for a balance that allows us to thrive without sacrificing our well-being. By navigating the fine line between ambition and destruction, we can lead fulfilling lives that are both successful and sustainable.

\*\*\*

As the days turned into weeks, and the weeks turned into months, Luxy Lox, my small business, was thriving. I was fortunate enough to see not just revenue, but profit. This newfound financial relief led me to desire a more luxurious life, causing me to neglect the growth of my teething business. I became selfish and indulged in the convenience of most especially, food delivery apps, ordering from upscale restaurants daily.

Oddly enough, even though I had access to home-cooked meals, I still craved the experience of ordering out. This unhealthy habit extended beyond food as I swiped my card for unnecessary coffees, snacks, and meals at swanky restaurants that had potential to drain my funds. I failed to realize in that moment that while I appeared to be profiting, I was actually incurring substantial losses due to my lifestyle choices. I was driven by the psychology of buying things simply because I could. Some would mistakenly label it as arrogance, when in reality, it was my inexperience shining through.

Being a sole trader, it was crucial for me to differentiate between personal and business expenses. I should have been allocating a monthly wage from the business's proceeds to fund my desired luxuries.

As an inexperienced trader, I failed to grasp the complexities of running a business effectively. I blurred the lines between personal and business finances, neglecting balance sheets, costs sheets, and stock lists.

The consequences of my actions soon unravelled. I struggled to meet the monthly payments to vendors, causing delays in fulfilling orders and ultimately losing valuable business. It became apparent that something needed to change before it reached a point of no return.

In realizing my miscalculations, I began to take the necessary steps towards rectifying the situation. I prioritized understanding the intricacies of my business by seeking guidance and education on financial management. I soon acknowledged the importance of separating personal and business finances, ensuring that the needs of the company were met before indulging in personal luxuries.

It was a humbling experience, realizing that success in business requires not only hard work but also discipline and financial intelligence. I learned that the allure of a polished life must be balanced with the sustainability and growth of my business. By implementing a more strategic approach and making informed financial decisions, I could have secured a successful future for Luxy Lox.

Sadly, without the right level of discipline, the structure of the trying business was at its wits end, leaving me in a situation where it was far too late.

# DRAWING   BOARD

When we make initial life choices that we believe make the most sense in that moment, we often believe that we are on the right path. This changes at some point thereafter. Somewhere in the middle of our journey, we find ourselves in a state of confusion and uncertainty. We make decisions that end up destroying the progress we have made and jeopardizing our future. In these moments, we are faced with a critical juncture, the angle point, where we must decide where to go next.

The angle point is a defining moment in our lives. It is the moment when we realize that the choices we have made so far have led us astray, and we are forced to confront the consequences of our actions. It is a pivotal moment that brings out our survival instincts, causing us to enter into the dreaded, yet useful, fight or flight mode. We tap into the deepest reserves of our strength and determination, utilizing resources and skills we were unaware we possessed. The angle point is where we take control of our lives, exerting energy and effort that we never knew we had.

At this point, we may feel overwhelmed and lost, unsure of where to turn or what steps to take next.

However, it is crucial that we acknowledge and learn from our mistakes. The angle point is an opportunity for reflection and growth. It is a chance to evaluate what went wrong and to identify the actions and decisions that led us off course. Byrecognizing our errors, we can ensure that we never make those same mistakes again.

Maturity becomes an integral part of our decision-making process at the angle point. We transition from inexperience to experience, gaining wisdom and insight along the way. This newfound maturity shapes our future decisions. We become more cautious, afraid of repeating past failures, and more calculated in navigating change and challenges. The angle point instils in us a sense of resilience and determination as we strive to rebuild our lives from the ground up.

In this critical juncture, it is important to remember that making mistakes is a part of being human. It is through these mistakes that we learn and grow. The angle point serves as a reminder that life is not always a straight path to fulfilment. It is filled with twists and turns, ups and downs, and unexpected obstacles. It is during these challenging moments that we discover our true strength and resilience. It is when we are faced with the destruction of our initial life choices, that we have the opportunity to rise above and forge a new path.

So, where do we go from the angle point? We go forward, armed with the lessons learned from our past mistakes. We take control of our lives and our decisions. We navigate the uncertain terrain with caution and maturity, ensuring that we make choices that align with our true values and aspirations.

The angle point becomes aturning point, a catalyst for growth and self-discovery. It may take time and effort to rebuild what was broken, but itis through this process that we become the architects of our own lives, creating a future that is shaped by our determination and resilience. Despite the destruction that may have occurred, it is through this process that we have the opportunity to rebuild and create a life that aligns with our true values. The angle point is not the end of our journey but a turning point that propels us towards a brighter future.

*\*\*\**

Eventually, my first business fizzled out due to my own negligence. Although a painful experience, the gloom did not accompany me for long; if anything, there was a yearning to learn more and start again.

When I embarked on my entrepreneurial journey, I was filled with optimism and a deep desire to create something meaningful. The idea of having my own business excited me and fuelled my determination. I had meticulously planned every aspect, from product development to marketing strategies. However, along the way, I let complacency creep into my actions.

As the weeks turned into months trying to stabilize Luxy Lox, I got caught up in the insignificant operations of the business. I became too focused on the immediate tasks at hand, neglecting the bigger picture. I failed to adapt to changing market trends and failed to stay ahead of my competition. My once-thriving business soon faced the stark reality of decline. The downfall of my venture hit me hard. I was disheartened and felt an overwhelming sense of failure.

Instead of dwelling in self-pity, I decided to reflect on the lessons this experience had taught me. It was in this period of introspection that I discovered my true passion for entrepreneurship and my yearning to learn more and start over.

I began to analyse the mistakes I had made and the areas where I had fallen short. I realized that business is not just about having a unique idea but also about constant improvement, adaptability, and resilience. With newfound determination, I enrolled in business courses, attended workshops, and devoured every book on entrepreneurship I could find.

As I delved into the world of business education, I learned the importance of continuous learning and staying abreast of industry trends. I discovered the value of networking and surrounding myself with like-minded individuals who could provide me with guidance and support. Gradually, the gloom of my previous failure lifted, replaced by a renewed sense of purpose and a burning desire to succeed.

Armed with knowledge and a fresh perspective, I decided to give my entrepreneurial dreams another try. This time, I approached my venture with a strategic mindset, mindful of the challenges that lay ahead. I developed a comprehensive business plan, focused on building a strong team, and embraced innovation.

Though the fear of failure lingered in the back of my mind, I refused to let it paralyze me. Instead, I used it as a driving force, propelling me to work harder and smarter. I understood that setbacks were part of the journey and that even the most successful entrepreneurs had experienced failure.

In the end, the failure of my first business proved to be a blessing in disguise.

***

In 2018, amidst warm, sunny weather in Nairobi, I found myself immersed in a new environment. Having arrived merely two days earlier, I began acquainting myself with the distinctive architecture that adorned the city.
My desire to travel was driven not by the allure of luxury, as many would presume, but rather by the prospect of gaining a fresh perspective. I sought solace in the knowledge that there existed a world beyond my four-bedroom walls; a world beyond the confines of the one-mile radius surrounding my local supermarket; and most importantly, a world beyond the borders of the country I called home.

Traveling has always been an escape for me, a means of stepping away from the familiar, and immersing myself in the unknown. It represents an opportunity to break free from the monotony of everyday life and explore the vast wonders that lie beyond. While some may view travel as a mere leisure activity, for me, it acts as a lens through which I can see the world with a broader perspective.

Nairobi, with its vibrant culture and intricate architecture, was just the beginning of my journey. The moment I stepped foot in the city, I was captivated by its charm and uniqueness. Every street corner unveiled a new story, and every building whispered tales of the past. As I wandered the bustling streets, from the magnificent Maasai Market to the historic Nairobi Railway Museum, I couldn't help but feel a deep sense of awe and curiosity for the world that lay beyond.

The warmth of the sun beaming down on me seemed to ignite a fire within, fuelling my desire to explore further and seek out new experiences. This revelation heightened my awareness that there was so much more to discover, not just in Nairobi, but in every corner of the globe. It was this awareness that became my driving force, igniting a passion for travel that I knew would shape my future endeavours.

Travel affords individuals the privilege of peeling back the layers of their own limited existence, allowing them to forge connections with people and cultures that are vastly different from their own. It provides an opportunity to experience the world in all its diversity, and in turn, foster a deeper understanding and appreciation for humanity as a whole.

As I embarked on my new adventure, I encountered individuals whose lives were shaped by circumstances starkly different from my own. In their stories, I found a wellspring of compassion that reminded me of the shared humanity that binds us all. Whether it was engaging in heartfelt conversations with locals in the bustling markets of Gikomba, or witnessing the resilience of individuals striving for a better future in Kibera, each encounter served as a gentle reminder that there is so much more to the world than what immediately meets the eye.

By venturing beyond the confines of my immediate environment, I constantly challenged my preconceived notions and gradually expanded my worldview. I came to realize that the problems and struggles faced by individuals were not confined to a specific geographic location, but were shared by people around the globe.

Poverty, inequality, and injustice were not exclusive to any country, but rather universal challenges that required a collective effort to overcome.

Globetrotting had granted me the privilege of living simultaneously within the realm of my own reality and the world at large. It taught me that there is no substitute for the first-hand knowledge gained through personal experiences and interactions. It equally reminded me that even within the comfort of my own home, I can continue to grow and learn by embracing an open mind and seeking out opportunities for cultural exchange.

As the warm, sunny day in Nairobi drew to a close, I knew that my journey had only just begun. The architecture that initially captivated me was merely a precursor to the many wonders I would encounter along the way. Travel had become my safe haven, my window into the vastness of the world. It had provided me with the solitude of knowing that there was more, much more, beyond the familiar confines of my daily life. And with each new adventure, I was privileged to gain a deeper appreciation for the beautiful tapestry of humanity that envelops our world.

***

Exploring new cities every few months became a constant at that point in my life, giving Nairobi - at that time - the title of my favourite.
"Habari yako?" graced my ears from the locals with every outing I made, instantly giving me a sense of relief that it wasn't the typical no-greeting misery that often presented itself in the not-so-sunny England. There was a peace that came with being in Nairobi, giving me the confidence to fit right in with the crowd.

Sitting by the window of my Kilimani apartment, I sipped on a very hot masala tea, followed by a gracious bite of the perfectly shaped, fluffy mandazi. It was at that moment that I realized everything I had been through prior was all worth it. What I was doing in that moment, was worth it. I was following a path that was destined for me. That simple moment rewarded me an encouraging sense of gratitude, one that still lives inside of me till this very day.

As I sat in front of my laptop, engulfed in the whirlwind of information flowing through cyberspace, a striking headline caught my eye: 'Kenya Quickly Becoming Africa's Tech Hub.' Immediately, a surge of excitement coursed through my veins, and my mind was a flurry of thoughts.

The notion that Kenya was swiftly emerging as a technological powerhouse immediately captured my attention. I realized that with this newfound development, there must be immense potential for new and existing businesses in the African market. As I delved deeper into my research, I recognized a significant gap in the African market – the absence of a comprehensive platform dedicated to covering African news focusing on innovative tech start-ups; another, facilitating hiring services through e-commerce.

Drawing upon my knowledge in information technology, acquired through years of personal and professional endeavours, I realized I had the skills necessary to bridge this gap. It was a moment of epiphany, a moment when my passions for business and technology converged seamlessly.

The memory of my previous venture, where I had failed to do sufficient research and establish valuable connections -

loomed large in my mind. Now armed with the lessons learned from my past failure, I resolved to embark on this new adventure with renewed vigour.

\*\*\*

Engrossing myself with many hours of extensive research, it was clear that I had to find out more. Web searches offered me so much, yet so little. I needed human interaction.

As I sat in the backseat of the taxi, anxiously anticipating my arrival at a 6pm Lavington event, I couldn't help but reflect on the significance of this moment. Engaging with others within the same field as me was a decision I had pondered over for quite some time. It meant stepping out of my comfort zone and exposing myself to unfamiliar territory. I had grown tired of being isolated in my pursuits and realized the importance of connecting with like-minded individuals.

Securing the strap on my right high heel, seemingly in a moment of angst, I meticulously made sure everything was in place. In those last few minutes of the car ride, I reaffirmed my commitment to facing my anxieties head-on. Time seemed to be in my favour as I glanced at my watch and realized I was slightly ahead of schedule. I smiled at the thought of my preference for being early rather than late. It was a small victory, but it gave me a glimmer of confidence.

Arriving at the event venue precisely at 5.46pm, I stepped out of the taxi and took a deep breath.

The grandness of the venue and the presence of elites filled the air with majesty and importance.

I could feel the weight of the occasion press upon me, but I refused to let it overwhelm me.

As I made my way towards the entrance, I reminded myself of the purpose behind my decision to engage with others in my field. It was about fostering connections, exchanging ideas, and broadening my horizons. The discomfort I felt was merely a reminder of the potential growth that lay ahead.

Walking into the room, I noticed familiar faces mingling with unfamiliar ones. The chatter of animated conversations filled the space, creating an atmosphere of intellectual stimulation. My nerves settled as I recognized the common passion that united everyone in that room.

Embracing the uncertainty, I began to engage with others, initiating conversations and actively listening to their experiences. The initial discomfort that had plagued me earlier transformed into a catalyst for personal and professional growth. I realized that the anxiety I once tried to avoid was, in fact, a motivation to push myself further.

Throughout the evening, I found myself immersed in discussions and debates, exchanging ideas and building connections. Conversing with various individuals, I discovered how much I could learn from them and how much they could learn from me. It was a realization that reinforced the importance of engaging with others in a similar field.

Shortly after the cocktail hour, the attendees were ushered to their seats for the introductory presentation, followed by the panellist discussion.

Again, familiar faces sat on the centre stage in front of me, leaving me eager to take notes as an awestruck attendee and ready to imitate their tricks in the game.

As the discussion unfolded, I couldn't help but immerse myself in the inspiring stories shared by successful entrepreneurs and tech experts. The room was buzzing with excitement and enthusiasm, leaving us all captivated by the wealth of knowledge and experience surrounding me. It was in that moment, amidst the energy and passion, that I realized the power of networking and seizing opportunities.

After the event, I mustered up the courage to approach some of the panellists and introduce myself. I shared my idea for an e-commerce platform catering to African tech start-ups and hiring services, hoping to garner their interest and gather insights. To my surprise, they not only listened intently but also expressed their support and offered valuable advice, eventually exchanging contact details.

The warmth and receptiveness of the Nairobi tech community was truly unparalleled.
It was time. A new energy filled my body to outshine myself, to recreate myself.

To make use of the drawing board.

# RECREATION

New energy is a force that permeates through every aspect of our lives. It is that feeling of hope, excitement, and motivation that propels us forward towards our goals and aspirations. When this new energy manifests, it creates a shift in our lives - a positive transformation that can be both invigorating and daunting. However, this shift often incites ill-intentioned individuals to prey on those who are undergoing personal growth.

During a significant life transition, there is an inherent vulnerability that arises. As we navigate uncharted territories and explore new possibilities, it becomes vital to be aware of our surroundings and the people we interact with. Not everyone will be able to comprehend or celebrate this newfound energy, and it is in these instances that ill intentions tend to rear their ugly heads. Whether intentional or unintentional, these individuals may attempt to sabotage our progress and undermine our judgement.

It is crucial to stay attuned to our intuition and recognize any signs of bad will directed towards us. This requires strength and self-awareness. If we are not vigilant, these ill-intentioned individuals can easily knock us off balance, causing doubt, confusion, and even derailing our progress.

Therefore, it is imperative to develop resilience and fortitude in order to navigate this treacherous terrain and protect our newfound positive energy.

In times of setbacks or challenges, recreating ourselves becomes a necessity for maintaining our mental stability. When faced with adversity, it is crucial to reflect on our experiences and learn from them. Through introspection, we can develop a clearer understanding of what we truly desire and meticulously plan how to achieve it. This process of self-recreation allows us to refine our goals, align them with our newfound energy, and create a roadmap for success.

While recreating ourselves after a setback, we become more in tune with our values, passions, and purpose. We gain clarity of mind and unwavering determination to pursue our ambitions. With this renewed sense of self, we are better equipped to detect and deflect ill intentions that may come our way. Our strengthened line of judgement serves as a shield, preventing negativity from infiltrating our journey towards growth and self-actualization.

New energy is a powerful force that transforms our lives for the better. It equally attracts spiteful individuals who may seek to impede our progress. Recognizing this, it is essential to stay vigilant and develop the strength to protect our line of judgement. Recreating ourselves after setbacks allows us to align our goals with our newfound energy and fortify our mental stability. By doing so, we become resilient individuals capable of shielding ourselves from negativity and navigating the path to personal growth with confidence and clarity.

\*\*\*

Getting back to my apartment late at night with a new sense of enlightenment felt incredible. Every aspect of my surroundings appeared refreshed, including myself. It felt as if a burden had been lifted off my shoulders, an evening that I had yearned for without realizing it. After freshening up, I sat down at my desk and powered up my laptop, going back to what I had earlier been researching.

Driven by my passion for technology, I decided to begin piecing together and code a website that would connect regional consumers with media professionals, catering to both their online and offline needs. It was a service-based platform influenced by the ever-evolving tech industry. Excited and determined, I began reaching out to potential clients that I had met earlier via email, convincing them that they could benefit from the services my new venture offered. Soon enough, I started receiving responses.

As I lay in bed that night, fully aware that this journey wouldn't be easy, especially for a young woman navigating the complexities of business, I knew that giving up was not an option. The thrill of the challenge energized me, exercising my determination to succeed.

Days passed, and I diligently worked on launching my websites. One catered to news within the African tech market, another focused on connecting media professionals, and a third offered car hire services – all under the umbrella of a single business group. The moment I announced these services, my phone buzzed incessantly with potential leads. It was at that very moment that I realized I was back on track.
Still mindful of the setback I had experienced previously, I couldn't rely solely on this new venture. I understood the importance of diversifying my investments and seeking alternate sources of income.

Consequently, I delved into extensive research on how to invest in small start-up companies. Immersed in profiles and frameworks, I eventually identified a UK-based tech start-up that showed immense promise. Confident in its potential for rapid growth, I decided to invest a modest four-figure sum. It was a calculated risk, but one that I believed would yield significant returns in the coming months.

Fortunately, my instincts turned out to be correct, and before I knew it, I held shares in the company. Though the value of my investment may have been small and seemingly insignificant, it symbolized a noteworthy step forward in my entrepreneurial journey. It demonstrated my commitment to seizing opportunities and being a part of the ever-expanding tech industry.

This series of events had reignited my entrepreneurial spirit. It reminded me of the importance of perseverance, resilience, and the willingness to adapt and explore new avenues. It was a reawakening, a reminder that even in the face of setbacks, success was attainable with determination and an unwavering belief in one's abilities.

As I closed my eyes that night, after many long nights, thoughts of the future danced in my mind. I knew that the path ahead would be challenging, but also fuelled by a renewed sense of purpose, coupled with a burning desire to make a lasting impact in the entrepreneurial world. This journey was far from over. With the experiences gained and the wisdom acquired, I was ready to conquer new horizons and face whatever obstacles lay ahead.

# THE LONG GAME

In today's fast-paced and highly competitive business world, it has become increasingly crucial for entrepreneurs to be able to work on their new ventures diligently, without making silly errors. It is no longer enough to have a great product or service; one must also be able to navigate the financial aspects of the business and effectively manage personal and professional profits and losses. Making use of useful information both online and offline to refrain from profoundly creating financial errors, have become indispensable to thrive in the modern marketplace.

First and foremost, a key aspect of running a successful business is being able to update the profit and loss, and balance sheet regularly. These financial documents serve as a snapshot of the company's financial health and helps to make informed decisions.
It is essential to accurately track expenses and income, ensuring that costs are appropriately allocated, and profits are properly recognized. By diligently updating this document, entrepreneurs can identify areas of weakness, make informed financial decisions, and maximize the profitability of their new business.

Moreover, keeping personal and professional profits and losses separate is vital to the long-term success of the enterprise. Mixing personal and business finances can lead to confusion, potential legal issues, and the loss of credibility in the eyes of clients and investors.

For many businesses, especially those operating as legal entities such as limited liability companies (LLCs) or corporations, maintaining separate bank accounts is often a legal obligation. These legal entities are distinct from their owners, and commingling personal and professional finances can jeopardize this legal separation. By adhering to this requirement, entrepreneurs protect themselves and their businesses from complications, maintaining the integrity and separate identities of both personal and professional finances. This compliance with legal requirements establishes a solid foundation for business growth and expansion by demonstrating professionalism and responsibility to potential investors, partners, and creditors.

The separation of personal and professional bank accounts also has practical implications in day-to-day business operations. It simplifies bookkeeping and accounting processes, making financial record-keeping more efficient and accurate. This simplification saves entrepreneurs valuable time and effort that can be directed towards more critical aspects of running their businesses.

*\*\**

During the course of the months, I had ensured that – learning from previous mistakes – all of my personal income and expenses were completely separated from proceeds the business collected and spent.

Sometimes I would go as far as to use my own personal income to re-inject into the business, sacrificing my personal happiness for the betterment of the company. As much as this was wrong, as balance is truly the key to a better life, in my eyes it was the completely right thing to do. Absolutely, without hesitation.

I realized whilst on my vacation in Nairobi however, that there was a need for me to be social. I did deserve good people around me; people also deserved for me to be a good person to them. It didn't take long after posting on my social media platforms that I was in the locality, that a few lost friends decided to reach out, which felt good as a sense of relief that I wasn't forgotten.

In 2018-2019, I found myself alternating between Kenya and the UK; an experience, undoubtedly, that I will never forget. It was in this environment that I discovered a whole new dimension of living when I ventured out of my comfort zone. Being surrounded by individuals who were constantly pushing themselves and juggling multiple responsibilities inspired me to do the same. The work ethic I witnessed in Nairobi left an indelible mark on me, teaching me the value of hard work and perseverance.

One aspect of Kenyan culture that played a surprising role in my journey towards achieving work-life balance was the food. The wholesome aroma of nyama choma, sukuma, and ugali often greeted me in the evenings, providing a much-needed respite from the hustle and bustle of the day. These simple yet delicious dishes became a source of comfort and fuel, giving me the energy I needed to keep going. Taking a break to enjoy a meal became a ritual that helped me stay focused and refreshed.

Of course, finding a work-life balance is never easy, and there were many sleepless nights spent planning and strategizing, but unlike previous experiences, this period of my life felt surprisingly manageable. The challenges I faced in 2016, when I first embarked on this journey, had prepared me for the hurdles I encountered in Kenya. I had grown accustomed to the demands of a busy lifestyle, and I knew that if I could handle it once before, I could do it again.

9.45pm, East Africa Time (EAT), I closed my eyes for the last time in a long time on Kenyan soil before a new journey I didn't know I would be taking.

# EXPLORATION

In today's globalized world, the pace in which technology evolved is still steadily accelerating. While developed economies have readily embraced these advancements, developing economies often struggle to keep up. It is essential for entrepreneurs to thoroughly study the market before venturing into these new territories, as the environment may present unique challenges and opportunities. By immersing themselves in different cultures through travel, individuals gain valuable insights into what is lacking and what is thriving. This knowledge can greatly benefit entrepreneurs, allowing them to incorporate these findings into their business strategies.

As I personally experienced during my travels to South Sudan in 2020, I discovered that this developing economy was particularly conducive to product-based businesses due to its relatively unsaturated market, and demand for cash-in-hand transactions.

One of the primary advantages of exploring developing economies is observing the gaps in technology and business ventures. These regions often lack access to state-of-the-art technology, efficient infrastructure, and modernized business practices.

This scarcity also presents opportunities for entrepreneurs to introduce innovative solutions tailored to the specific needs of the population. By gaining a first-hand understanding of the limitations and challenges faced by individuals in these communities, business-minded individuals can develop products and services that cater to their unique requirements. Understanding these gaps is fundamental in building successful businesses that can make a positive impact on the local community.

Traveling provides entrepreneurs with a unique perspective that cannot be obtained through mere research or analysis. While studying market reports and conducting surveys are vital steps in market research, they only provide a partial understanding of the local dynamics. Immersing oneself in the local culture fosters a deeper understanding of the people's preferences, lifestyles, and aspirations. It allows entrepreneurs to perceive the nuances and intricacies of the market, enabling them to identify and seize untapped opportunities successfully. By traveling to developing economies like South Sudan, entrepreneurs gain an invaluable experience, developing a sharper mind that allows them to uncover hidden potential within the market.

My journey to South Sudan reiterated the potential for product-based businesses in a relatively untapped market. The economic landscape of this country showcased an absence of the saturation commonly seen in developed economies, such as the United Kingdom. This presented a unique advantage for entrepreneurs looking to introduce and establish their product-based businesses. The reduced competition allowed for greater visibility and market penetration, giving entrepreneurs a better chance of carving out a niche and building a loyal customer base.

By recognizing this distinction and adapting their business strategies accordingly, entrepreneurs can take advantage of these opportunities to prosper in developing economies.

Developing economies often take a slower stance when it comes to adopting technology and exploring new business ventures; but it is this delay can present unique advantages for entrepreneurs who possess a keen eye for market potential. These travel experiences provide invaluable knowledge that can be incorporated into business strategies, ultimately leading to successful ventures. My own exploration of South Sudan highlighted the promising landscape for business. By recognizing and capitalizing on these opportunities, entrepreneurs can flourish in these developing economies, creating not only successful enterprises but also bringing about positive change in the local community.

***

2020.

"Where is your final destination, Miss?". I found myself at the Border Control zone leaving Kenya into Uganda. I accompanied my brother-in-law to South Sudan via Uganda, as he was also in Kenya at the time I was there. I was fuelled with excitement, but also a profound nervousness, as it will be my first time back to South Sudan after a gruelling five years away. Even then, five years prior, I rarely went outdoors as I was terribly home sick.

As we got our entry visa to Uganda stamped, it felt surreal that so much was happening in my life at a fast pace. The anxiety was somehow exhilarating, giving me the power I needed to quickly tap into fight or flight mode -

the exact energy I needed to excel in the environment I would eventually delve into.

The three-day transit in Kampala was relaxing. Although not leaving the apartment, I could sense that the locals were welcoming and ready to execute first class hospitality to all foreigners.

The bustling city of Kampala offered a unique blend of modernity and tradition. The skyscrapers stood tall, showcasing the rapid development of the country, while the traditional markets and cultural sites reminded visitors of Uganda's rich heritage. Each day, I would catch glimpses of this vibrant city through the window, eager to explore its streets and immerse myself in its culture.

The first day in Kampala, I slept. The second day was productive, however. The apartment complex was massive, with multiple outdoor sections each providing different services catering to not only residents, but for locals wanting to host events of any capacity.

For me to tap into the African market, it would make sense to mingle with the staff to see where my company's services could come in handy. If this was when I first started out in business, my inability to speak in social settings would have not allowed me to confidently be seated in the Events Manager's office four hours into the new day, discussing how my company could partner with them, and how greatly they could benefit from the services provided.

It took one cup of water, two listening ears, a very well-versed impersonal pitch, a handshake, and a paper to sign to get a partnership under way; ready to complete once I get back to the United Kingdom.

In this very moment, I didn't realize that I would not be going back to the UK for another two years.

Upon arrival at our final destination, South Sudan, I felt a feeling I had never felt before. I couldn't quite understand what the feeling was. Maybe I needed to get some sleep? Perhaps knowing that it was my parents' resting place for once made me slow down and take a long hard look at reality? Till this day, I will never quite understand what that feeling was and why I felt it.

As we drove through various towns within South Sudan, we finally arrived in Juba, the capital city. There was still a lingering sense of apprehension. I wondered if I would be able to adapt to the challenges that awaited me, or if I could contribute to the country's economic progression. After sorting out my sim-card and settling into the apartment, I finally slept for what felt like decades. It wasn't in fact decades; it was only thirty minutes.

Have you ever woken up and had an instant hit of anxiety, especially when you're in an unfamiliar environment, completely out of your comfort zone, with majority of your closest friends and family thousands of miles away? The dryness in your throat when you have a 'what in the world did I do' moment? That was me. Deep down I knew that the inevitable was to happen – going to my parents' grave site, which left me with an unsettling feeling deep down in my gut. The phone call that followed, solidified that feeling of knowing that it was time to get ready and leave.
Do I wear black, or should I wear a coloured outfit? Do I need to wrap my hair? The endless list of questions filled my head. Questions that I already knew the answers to, yet overthinking every detail that wasn't completely necessary.

We got to Bilpham at 3pm. I still remember that day as being worse than the funeral itself. One could say that mourning as a pre-teen is a lot easier than mourning as an adult, and I can attest to that. I almost refused to get out of the car as my nerves began to control every fibre of my body; but even worse, walking towards the graves felt like hell. It was the realization that I was not hoping for - that the line between life and death was so thin. That a few feet under the heavily mounted tombstones, lay the bodies of my lifeless parents.

I laid my roses, asked for their protection, and left.

The first few weeks in South Sudan were a whirlwind of emotions and adjustments. I reconnected with old friends and family members, sharing stories and laughter. We reminisced about the past and discussed our hopes and dreams for the future. It was heartening to see the resilience and determination of the people, who were rebuilding their lives despite the hardships they had endured.

As I settled into my new life in South Sudan, I realized that my vision of the country was evolving. It was no longer just a place where I had holidayed as a child; it was a place that held immense potential and opportunities. I saw the determination in the eyes of young people, eager to learn and contribute to their communities. I saw the resilience of women, who were fighting for equality and empowerment. I saw the passion of artists and entrepreneurs, who were using their creativity and innovation to drive change.

Juba got progressively easier for me to navigate around. It was there that I put the social skills I had developed in Nairobi into action.

Attending events, yet still being able to maintain my mysterious demeanour, it quickly became apparent to people that I was there for business. Although not being in South Sudan for several years put me at an initial disadvantage, I quickly worked my way up, broadening my horizon at every opened opportunity I got.
It wasn't long after settling in, that I formally registered my company there, seemingly easier as a dual citizen of the country.

Progressively, I got the key to my office space and filled it with staff, realizing with time that this whole setup made orchestrating business deals smoother.
Something I noticed almost immediately being in Juba was the need for a physical location that your company was operating in for it to appear legitimate, as the use of technology at that point was still a new thing. The idea that one could not only work from home, but also make sales from the comfort of their bedroom with just phone alerts, was not entirely recognized by the majority. Doing things that way would've slowed down productivity massively, proving the longevity of my stay there to be a waste of time.

The suitcase that I had packed for just a two-week stay, had become empty within days; either meaning I ran through my clothes quicker than I had anticipated, or I stayed longer than the two weeks I initially planned for. It was the latter.

February 2020 turned into December 2020 and before I knew it, Juba quickly became home. I quickly learned the disparities living in a fast-paced city, where things can turn around for you in a very short period.

You rest too hard, you lose business; you work too hard, you end up ill having to take bed rest and losing out anyway. Perhaps it was the fast pace that kept me going, challenging myself again and again until I was no longer fearful of… anything?
Socially, I was thriving, gracing me the opportunity of knowing a few heavyweights within the various industries that gradually presented themselves.
With a schedule filled with invitations, my network grew, giving me no choice but to stay a little while longer.

There was a humbling moment within the chaos of that year that proved to be disbelief. I had pushed myself over hurdles, through the fury of endless obstacles since my first 'self' discovery in 2016, that not much was going to intimidate me anymore. This wasn't for anyone else; it was for me to validate that from the very beginning of realizing I had a gift, I was able to action it. It was belief within myself, and continually believing in myself, that had got me that far.

December 15th, 2020. The sun had disappeared from the horizon, welcoming the evening bustle. It was then, that an unwavering sense of humility clouded any insignificant thought I had. Slowly bending my head and cupping my face, a sealed whisper, "Thank you, God" left my mouth, a tear followed soon after.

2020 was a year of challenges and uncertainties, but it was also a year of resilience and hope. It was a year that reminded us of the power of community, of the importance of coming together to overcome adversity. As I reflect on my journey back to South Sudan, I am filled with a renewed sense of purpose and determination. I am ready to contribute to the development of my country, to be a part of its transformation.

My final destination may have been South Sudan, but my journey was just beginning. I was committed to working towards a brighter future, where all its citizens have access to basic services and opportunities for growth. I strongly believe that together, we can build a stronger, more prosperous South Sudan.

As I look ahead to the future, I am reminded of the words of Nelson Mandela, who said, "Education is the most powerful weapon which you can use to change the world." It is with this belief that I will embark on my journey, armed with knowledge, compassion, and a desire to make a difference.

# FU LFI LM EN T

At this point in your business, where it has taken off and everything seems to have fallen into place, there is undoubtedly a satisfying sense of fulfilment. Finally seeing the fruits of your labour and witnessing the success that you have worked so hard for can be immensely gratifying. However, it is crucial to remind yourself that the world of entrepreneurship is a never-ending school, constantly teaching you new lessons and presenting new challenges. It is important not to fall into the trap of complacency that the comfort of fulfilment can bring.

One common mistake that entrepreneurs often make is assuming that once they have achieved a certain level of success, they have reached the pinnacle of their learning journey. However, this couldn't be further from the truth.

The truth is, no matter how successful your business becomes, there will always be more to learn and discover. Business is an ever-evolving field, with new ideas, technologies, and strategies emerging constantly. Stagnation, therefore, is not an option.

Learning is an ongoing process that transcends monetary success.

Whether you earn two figures or six figures a month, there will always be something new to discover and explore. By embracing this mindset, you open yourself up to continuous growth and improvement, enabling your business to stay ahead in the ever-competitive marketplace.

The comfort of fulfilment can be enticing. It tempts you to relax, enjoy the fruits of your labour, and become complacent. If you succumb to this trap, your business may stagnate and lose the momentum it had gained. It is crucial to understand that business success is not a destination but a journey. It requires constant adaptation, innovation, and a hunger for knowledge.

Remaining in a perpetual state of learning and self-improvement is not only beneficial for your business, but also for your personal growth and development. By challenging yourself to continuously learn and improve, you will expand your knowledge base, develop new skills, and broaden your perspective. This will not only make you a more effective and efficient business leader but also enhance your decision-making abilities and overall success.

Embracing a mindset of constant learning will keep you agile and adaptable in an ever-changing business landscape. New technologies, consumer preferences, and market trends can completely reshape industries overnight. By remaining open to learning, you position yourself to take advantage of these changes and stay ahead of the curve.

Contentment is undoubtedly a cause for celebration and reflection on your victory; but it is essential not to allow this fulfilment to become a trap.

Business is a never-ending school, and it is crucial to remember that there is always more to learn and discover. By embracing a mindset of continuous learning and improvement, you ensure the longevity and success of your business while fostering personal growth and development. So, even when things seem to have fallen into place, never stop pursuing knowledge and growth in the limitless world of business.

***

"Take this to the pharmacy downstairs and take the dosage as advised". Ouch. The hustle and bustle finally caught up to me in what felt like the worst way. Getting to the hospital in itself felt like a painful chore, as the aches did not permit me to move an inch further than my bed. At this point in the UK, it would have most likely been a common cold or flu considering it was January, the heart of a wintery season. Far from this thought, it was clear that I was in a different continent with a completely different climate. It wasn't the common cold or the influenza virus that was attacking my body; it was malaria.

Eating became my least favourite thing to do, not to mention drinking water, as anything with too much or too little flavour would just come straight back out one way or the other. Sitting in the confines of my bedroom, helpless, I couldn't help but remember the last time I had malaria ten years prior. It dawned on me that I was still an amateur handling this type of illness, which felt like death itself.

"Ashrob moya sukun" was what I heard every morning when the housekeeper came into my room, noticing I was extremely unwell, in an innocent bid to help me; but unfortunately -

for me drinking hot water, as she had encouraged, was my worst nightmare, as it did a great job stirring up any digested food and aggressively bringing it out my mouth.

The bustling city I love, where dreams are made and opportunities abound, continued its relentless pace even as my business paused. It was a surreal feeling, a sinking realization that while life moved forward, I was stuck in a state of helplessness, fearing the loss of so much that I had worked tirelessly to build.

In those early days, when my phone rang constantly with new prospects and exciting collaborations, I never imagined a force stronger than my determination could halt the momentum. But here I was, witnessing the gradual decline in phone calls, the ebbing interest in what I had to offer. It was as if my vulnerability had shattered the perception of the 'strong and capable Aluel' that everyone had once known.

Curiosity, like a double-edged sword, swirled in the minds of those who had observed my transformation. Some reached out, driven by genuine concern and a desire to understand what had happened. They longed to offer support, to see if there was a way to resuscitate what once was. Their phone calls became lifelines, connecting me to a sense of normalcy as I laid in bed, counting the days to get back to full strength.

But not everyone indulged their curiosity. Some chose to stay silent, perhaps unsure of how to approach a situation that seemed so foreign to them. Their absence spoke volumes, leaving me to ruminate on the delicate nature of relationships, the impermanence of allegiances nurtured on business transactions and shared goals.

Weeks dragged on, each passing day blending into the next, an existence marred by uncertainty and doubt. Yet, nestled within the confines of my circumstance, there were moments of grace. With each new dawn, I found the strength to conduct the simpler tasks that once came effortlessly. It was a half-day working basis, a fraction of my former productivity, but it was progress nonetheless. Like a muted phoenix rising from the ashes, I sought solace in the small victories that kept me going.

It took me another month to ensure business was flowing at a controlled level, this time equipping my most trusted team members with the know-how on how to keep the company completely afloat in the instance that I was absent. Although my team were more than competent in being able to handle the office, I knew deep down that I was the only person that could run my company to the standard I felt it deserved. It's a normal feeling with anything you've babied from the ground-up.

\*\*\*

Believing that my life as I knew it was back in the direction that I had initially worked hard for, I was faced by the loom and gloom that had become a familiar presence in my life not so long ago, rearing its ugly head again two-months later. Malaria, the silent killer, had struck again, but this time with an intensity far greater than any I had experienced before. Coupled with the extreme exhaustion that had become a constant companion, I knew it was time to take a break - a long break, back to the UK.

Mentally, I believed I was unbreakable. The challenges life threw at me seemed surmountable, and I prided myself on my ability to persevere through even the toughest of times.

However, what I failed to realize was that life had a way of breaking you down physically if you consciously pushed yourself to the point of oblivion.

The symptoms of malaria were no strangers to me. I had experienced them before - the recurring fever, the chills that shook me to my core, the relentless fatigue that made even the simplest of tasks seem insurmountable. But this time, the symptoms hit me like a tidal wave, leaving me weak and helpless. The pain in my joints was unbearable, and it felt as if my body was slowly shutting down.

It was difficult for me to accept that I needed to take a step back, as the thought of leaving my work unfinished and waving goodbye to the people I had grown to care for was heart-wrenching. I had always prided myself on my unwavering commitment, and the idea of stepping away felt like a betrayal of that; but deep down, I knew that I couldn't continue to push myself in this state. It was time to prioritize my own well-being.

Returning to the UK was a bittersweet decision. On one hand, I longed for the familiarity of home, the comfort of being surrounded by loved ones who could provide the support I desperately needed. On the other hand, guilt gnawed at me, as I felt that my departure was abandoning those who relied on me. It was a battle within myself, between self-care and my sense of duty.

In hindsight, taking that much-needed break was the best decision I could have made. It would have allowed me the time and space to heal physically and regain some semblance of strength, and also offer me the opportunity to reflect and reassess my priorities.

I recognized that my physical and mental well-being were instrumental in enabling me to continue making a difference in the world. I needed to learn the importance of self-care and striking a balance between my personal needs and my desire to help others.

Sitting on an aeroplane again after what felt like a lifetime somehow gave me a bittersweet feeling of relief. It was devastating to leave what I successfully created from scratch behind, but it was a great feeling knowing that I was going back to the comfort of my bed in a territory that I was first-handily familiar with.

And there I was, head back, dehydrated and tired on my way back to London Heathrow Airport via Cairo on an EgyptAir aircraft. The journey home felt like a blur, mentally fighting for strength to get me back safely. The sun had just dipped below the horizon, painting the sky with hues of orange and pink. The exhaustion from my travels had started to take its toll, manifesting itself through a ravenous thirst that seemed unquenchable. As I sat, crammed into my airplane seat, surrounded by tired travellers, I couldn't help but reminisce about the amazing adventure I had just embarked upon.

The journey that awaited me was far from gentle. Having already spent countless hours on various modes of transportation, I knew it would be a battle of will and endurance to reach my final destination. The cacophony of noises and the constant hum of the plane's engines felt like a lullaby, slowly lulling me into a restless state of half-sleep. I fought to stay awake, afraid of slipping into a deeper slumber that could potentially disrupt my already fragile sleep cycle.

As the plane touched down in Cairo, reality hit me like a ton of bricks. I had a layover of only a few hours before I could board my connecting flight to London. My body ached, a combination of physical fatigue, malaria and the strain of constantly being on edge in a foreign country. The lukewarm water in my water bottle barely offered any respite from the growing dehydration that threatened to consume me.

The layover turned into a whirlwind of rushing through crowded hallways, navigating endless security checks, and desperately searching for nourishment. The airport, teeming with sleep-deprived passengers, offered a strange blend of excitement and misery that only travellers can truly understand. Time felt like an illusion, slipping through my fingers as I struggled to make sense of the chaotic environment around me.

Finally, as I boarded the plane that would take me back to London, I couldn't help but feel relief wash over me. Looking out the window, I watched as the city lights of Cairo faded away, leaving behind memories that would forever be etched in my mind. The exhaustion threatened to consume me, but the anticipation of returning home gave me a renewed sense of determination.

The last few hours of the flight were filled with a strange mix of exhaustion and anticipation. Despite the fatigue that had settled into my muscles, the thought of being reunited with loved ones and the familiarity of home provided me with the strength I needed to soldier on. The journey felt like a haze, a steady blur of clouds and flashing lights as the plane made its way through the night sky.

As London came into view with the twinkling lights welcoming me back, I felt a sense of accomplishment and gratitude gleam over me. The mental battle I had fought had tested my limits, pushing me to my breaking point and beyond. But I had made it through, still standing and ready to embrace the comforts of home.

Fulfilment, they say, is the ultimate goal in life. We are constantly taught to strive for success, to reach for the stars, and to never settle for anything less. And so, I found myself on an endless pursuit of fulfilment, believing that it would bring me immeasurable joy and contentment. Little did I know, however, that fulfilment could be the quietest thief of joy.

At a certain point in my life, I was completely consumed by the idea of achieving my goals. I became obsessed with what I didn't have, constantly yearning for more and never truly appreciating what I had already accomplished. It didn't matter how much progress I made or how many milestones I reached; it was never enough.

In my relentless pursuit of fulfilment, I failed to notice the small moments of joy that were right in front of me. The laughter shared with loved ones, the beauty of a sunset, the warmth of a hug - these seemingly insignificant moments were overshadowed by my perpetual desire for more. I was so fixated on what I thought would bring me happiness that I neglected the present moments that held true joy.

The more I sought after fulfilment, the more elusive it became. It was as if the joy I was seeking was constantly slipping through my fingers, leaving me empty and unfulfilled.

My happiness became contingent upon external factors - accomplishments, possessions, and recognition - rather than finding joy in the simple pleasures of everyday life.

It took being temporarily unwell to finally open my eyes to this truth. In a moment of physical weakness, I found myself reflecting on my life and the choices I had made. I realized that while I had achieved many of my goals, I had lost sight of the present, of the beauty that surrounded me. I had become so consumed by the pursuit of fulfilment that I had forgotten to live.

During those difficult days of recovery, I discovered that true joy resides not in the external world but within ourselves. It is in the moments of gratitude, mindfulness, and connection that we find genuine fulfilment. It is in appreciating what we have rather than focusing on what we lack that allows joy to flourish.

From that moment onward, I made a conscious effort to shift my mindset and approach life with gratitude and genuine humility. I began to acknowledge and celebrate the small victories, cherishing the moments that brought me happiness. I learned to find fulfilment in the simplest of things - a cup of coffee in the morning, a walk in the park, the laughter of friends.

Fulfilment, I learned, is not a destination to be reached but a state of being. It is an ongoing practice, a way of life. It is about finding contentment in the present and recognizing that joy is not always found in grand achievements but in the quiet moments that make up our everyday lives.

In the end, I realized that fulfilment is not the thief of joy itself but rather the pursuit of it.

# SETBACK

You may encounter another setback at this point, but it's important that you remember that setbacks are an inevitable part of life, regardless of the path we choose to follow. Surprisingly, it is quite rare for individuals to achieve success on their very first try. More often than not, one encounters numerous obstacles and failures before eventually striking gold. Whether it is in the realm of business or personal development, challenges will arise that will test the very limits of one's determination and perseverance. It is during these pivotal moments that many individuals contemplate giving up, as the losses and disappointments may seem insurmountable. It is essential to remember that experiencing setbacks is a natural and universal phenomenon.

In any pursuit, be it starting a new venture or embarking on a personal journey, encountering setbacks is almost inevitable. It is within these moments of difficulty that true character is shown and opportunities for growth and resilience present themselves. However, it is vital to recognize that success rarely comes easy, and more often than not, it requires persistence and the ability to learn from your failures.

It is natural for people to feel overwhelmed and disheartened. The burden of starting anew after substantial losses can be exhausting and demotivating. Many individuals may even question their ability to continue, as the temptation to give up looms over their heads. Yet, it is during these very moments that true strength must be summoned, for it is in persisting through adversity that success is ultimately achieved.

Giving up at the first signs of setback or failure is a trap that many fall into. It is easy to become disenchanted with the process, to believe that success should come quickly, effortlessly, and without any stumbling blocks. However, it is through the experience of failure that we grow and learn. Each setback offers valuable lessons and insights that can shape our future endeavours. It is these lessons that pave the way for future triumphs.

History is replete with examples of individuals who faced monumental setbacks but managed to rise above them and achieve greatness. Thomas Edison, the inventor of the light bulb, famously said, "I have not failed. I've just found 10,000 ways that won't work." Edison encountered countless obstacles and failures before finally discovering the solution to his invention. Similarly, J.K. Rowling, the creator of the Harry Potter series, faced numerous rejections from publishers before finally finding success. These individuals persisted despite setbacks and demonstrated unwavering determination, proving that perseverance and resilience are key components of success.

Setbacks are not only normal, but equally serve as opportunities for growth. They test our willingness to overcome challenges, push our limits, and foster resilience.

It is essential to embrace setbacks as a natural part of any journey and to recognize that success rarely comes without a few bruises along the way. The path to success may be littered with obstacles, but it is the lessons learned from these setbacks that ultimately shape our character and fuel our determination.

So, when faced with yet another setback, it is essential to remember that it is simply part of the journey. Giving up may seem tempting, but the rewards of persisting are immeasurable. The road to victory is paved with failures, and each setback brings us one step closer to our goals. Embrace the difficulties, learn from them, and rise stronger each time. Remember, luck rarely strikes on the first, second, or even third attempt. But persist, and you may just strike gold on your tenth.

\*\*\*

Living and working in South Sudan had exposed me to countless challenges, but none could compare to the fight against malaria. It was a battle that tested my physical and mental strength, and it was a battle I was determined to win.

The taxi ride home from the airport was a blur. My body felt weak, and my mind was overwhelmed with exhaustion. I couldn't help but doze off intermittently, seeking a temporary escape from the weariness that consumed me. The journey seemed to stretch on forever, each minute feeling like an eternity.

Upon arriving home, the aroma of freshly cooked stew filled the air. Normally, this would have been a source of warmth and nourishment for my weary soul, but even the smell of food made me feel nauseous.

It was a stark reminder of how much my body was struggling to fight off the malaria infection.

My family welcomed me, concern etched on their faces. They urged me to see a doctor, knowing that my stubbornness and determination often led me to neglect my own well-being. Reluctantly, I made the decision to contact my doctor's office, hoping for a same-day check-up.

Thankfully, luck was on my side, and I was able to secure a prompt appointment. I knew deep down that my condition was serious, and I needed immediate medical attention. The diagnosis came as no surprise - malaria, exhaustion, and dehydration. The doctor, with genuine concern, pleaded to transfer me to the hospital for an overnight stay in order to give my weakened body a chance to regain strength. However, my stubbornness and longing for the comfort of my own home led me to decline the offer.

Armed with the prescribed medication and precise instructions, I made my way back home. The thought of spending a night in a sterile hospital room was daunting. I knew that being in the familiar surroundings of home would aid in my recovery, if only mentally. As I settled into bed, the gravity of the situation began to sink in. This was not just another challenge to overcome; it was a battle against an invisible enemy that threatened my very existence.

Looking back at my time in Juba, I realized that fearlessness had become an integral part of my character. Living there had taught me to face adversity head-on, to tackle challenges without hesitation.

But this battle against malaria was different. It required patience, rest, and a willingness to let my body heal.

Over the next few days, as I embarked on my recovery, I found solace in the support of my family and friends. They reminded me of my strength, urging me not to let the debilitating effects of malaria define me. It was a long and arduous journey, but gradually, I began to regain my energy and vitality.

This experience was a humbling reminder of the fragility of the human body. It showcased the importance of taking care of oneself and not disregarding the signs of fatigue and exhaustion. It taught me that sometimes, the bravest decision one can make is to admit vulnerability and seek help.

I emerged from this battle with a newfound appreciation for the simple joys in life - the smell of food, the warmth of a loving embrace, and the strength of the human spirit. The temporary setback may have taken its toll on me, but it did not break me. It only served to reinforce my resilience and determination to overcome any obstacle life throws my way.

One could say a temporary decline in health would knock your confidence, but it didn't. Soon after my recovery, I made calls to my Accountant in Juba to see if everything was ok with the business, and whether I needed to come back within the following days. "No need, Boss", he replied. Resting me assured in his competence to streamline the company without my physical presence.

I knew then that I had a team I could trust, a team that could continue to deliver even in my absence.

This realization led to a newfound appreciation for the people around me - those who had believed in me, supported me, and worked alongside me to build something great.

As I returned to my daily life, I found myself noticing the little things that I had once taken for granted. The smell of food wafting from a local street vendor's cart, the taste of a perfectly brewed cup of coffee, the sound of laughter echoing through the air - these simple joys became reminders of the beauty and resilience of life.

Afterall, it wasn't just the sensory pleasures that I had come to appreciate. I also developed a deeper understanding of the power of love and connection. The warmth of a loving embrace, whether it was from a family member, a friend, a team member, or even a stranger, provided strength during the most challenging moments. It reminded me that we are not meant to navigate life's obstacles alone, but rather together, supporting one another despite temporary knocks.

# REDISCOVERY

There will be many moments when unforeseen circumstances can unexpectedly hit us like a ton of bricks. Whether it be falling ill or enduring a shocking situation, these occurrences have the power to disrupt our regular routine and force us to take a step back. It is in these moments of crisis that it becomes crucial for us to find equilibrium between rest and reflection. How we respond to these challenges can determine whether we emerge stronger or find ourselves spiralling down a dangerous path.

When hit by illness or a shocking situation, our first instinct is often to fight against it and get back on our feet as quickly as possible. This reaction is driven by a desire to regain control over our lives and remedy the discomfort that has befallen us. However, in our haste to reclaim normalcy, we may once again, forget the importance of rest and reflection.

Rest is not merely about physical recovery, but also mental and emotional restoration. When we are ill or shocked, our body and mind are vulnerable, and pushing ourselves beyond our abilities can do more harm than good.

It is during these moments of respite that we can gain clarity and perspective on the situation at hand.

This reflective period allows us to assess our actions leading up to the setback to identify areas where we went wrong. It is an opportunity for introspection and self-discovery, enabling us to learn from our mistakes and prevent similar occurrences in the future.

It is crucial to strike a balance and not allow excessive introspection to consume us. Many individuals, in an attempt to rectify their flaws or prove their resilience, become consumed by a new-found drive. This drive, fuelled by the disappointment and pain of previous let-downs, can push us to overexert ourselves and overcommit. In this state of frenzy, we forget the caution learned from our moment of crisis and dive headfirst into new challenges, ignoring the risks associated with overexertion.

Overdoing it can lead to exhaustion, burnout, and even further setbacks. When our bodies and minds are not given sufficient time to heal properly, we decrease our chances of fully recovering. Additionally, overexertion can cloud our judgment and cause us to make hasty decisions, resulting in detrimental outcomes. It is essential to be conscious of our limitations and respect the healing process.

Finding the right balance between rest and reflection is key. While rest allows us to recharge our physical and mental energy, reflection enables us to identify our shortcomings and develop strategies for improvement. Both elements work in harmony to create a solid foundation for personal growth and overall well-being.

The shock of a setback forces us to reconsider our approach to life and confront our vulnerabilities. It is in these moments that rest and reflection are pivotal, providing us with an opportunity to assess our past actions and identify areas that need immediate evaluation. By striking a balance between rest and reflection, we can emerge stronger and wiser, equipped with the insights necessary to navigate life's challenges more effectively.

***

Frequenting calls to Juba enabled me to have almost full control of the company without me needing to physically be there. This proved to be a significant advantage for the next step in my entrepreneurial expansion and personal progression.

As an ambitious individual, I have always been gifted with the entrepreneurial spirit to constantly focus on expansion; but I was faced with a challenge - the need to be physically present in Juba after a short time away, while also seeking opportunities in various other locations. This dilemma could have hindered my progress, but instead, it became a catalyst for innovation and growth.

Through the power of technology and constant communication, I was able to stay connected with my team in Juba. Regular calls allowed me to guide them, make important decisions, and contribute to the company's strategy. Despite the temporary physical distance, I felt a sense of control that reassured me about the direction we were heading in. This not only allowed me to manage the day-to-day affairs of the company, but it also gave me the opportunity to work on other aspects of my entrepreneurial adventure.

It provided me with the freedom to explore new ideas, expand my network, and seek partnerships that could potentially accelerate growth.

During this time, I had a realization that life waits for no one. Opportunities are fleeting, and it is up to us to seize them in order to prosper. This epiphany served as a driving force, igniting a zeal within me to do more and achieve greater heights. I understood that in order to build a lasting legacy and accumulate wealth, I needed to be proactive and take calculated risks.

Without hesitation, I began to draft an idea that had lingered in the back of my mind for a long time - the birth and invention of Aluel Deng, the brand. I had a clear vision of how I wanted it to be - an upscale brand that would captivate the hearts of individuals seeking luxury items. From clothing to Arabian perfume oils, leather handbags to silk scarves, Aluel Deng was to be the epitome of elegance and style, meticulously crafted and executed by me.

I researched, designed, and developed products that would embody the essence of luxury. I worked with artisans, designers, and suppliers to ensure that every aspect of the brand met my exacting standards.

The combination of technology, determination, and creative commitment allowed me to launch the brand with pride and confidence. Although physically absent from Juba, I knew that my new venture's influence had an impact on the first company's success.

As I continued to progress through my entrepreneurial journey, I was grateful for this transformative phase.

It taught me the value of adaptability, the power of technology in facilitating remote operations, and the significance of seizing opportunities to achieve longevity in wealth and security.

I knew that in order to remain relevant in the industry, it was crucial for me to maintain a strong social presence. As the global lockdown began to ease and businesses started to reopen, I considered myself fortunate to have the opportunity to visit the factories where my first products were being produced. These factories, although small, operated efficiently and were home to a village of highly skilled workers.

Being a perfectionist in my approach to business, it was a challenge for me to trust others to deliver exceptional results. However, the commitment and dedication displayed by these workers towards creating high-quality products to my liking, pleasantly surprised me. Time and time again, they exhibited an unwavering determination to meet and exceed expectations.

Despite the successful launch of my products, I recognized the need to allocate a portion of the profit from the other business towards the growth and expansion of my brand. I meticulously assessed the financial aspects of my business model and concluded that a larger advertising budget was crucial at this stage. I prioritized investing in stock and advertisement, realizing that an office space, especially in a city like London, was not a necessity at that moment. Other expenses seemed insignificant compared to the need to promote the brand in the highly competitive market.

Fortunately, I had reached a point where I was managing my business at its fullest capacity without experiencing excessive stress.

The products were being manufactured and shipped to me consistently, enabling me to successfully create a media and consumer presence. The positive response and feedback I received encouraged me to add more items to the stock list, expanding my product range and appealing to a broader customer base.

As I continued to navigate the intricacies of entrepreneurship, I recognized that remaining relevant in the industry requires constant adaptation and innovation. Keeping a high social presence was vital to ensure that my brand remained in the spotlight and continued to attract new customers. I understood that in order to grow and thrive, I needed to stay attuned to market trends and consumer preferences, always seeking opportunities to enhance my products and expand my reach. With a focus on adaptation and innovation, I remained committed, ultimately propelling my brand towards destined success.

# SOLITUDE

Congratulations, you've made it to a level of complete solitude. This is a tremendous milestone in your journey, where you have experienced the highs and lows, surpassed your own expectations and shattered countless self-doubts. In this moment of solitude, as an entrepreneur, you have the opportunity to both further expand your knowledge, and grow both personally and professionally.

By now, you have gained the invaluable experience of making substantial amounts of money. Your journey has taught you the taste of success and the rewards that come with it. You may have also experienced the bitter pill of loss, witnessing how easily everything you have built can crumble. These contrasting experiences have provided you with profound insights into the unpredictable nature of the business world.

Through these triumphs and defeats, you have developed a deep understanding of your capabilities, vulnerabilities, and strengths. In this solitude, you can objectively identify your weaknesses without hesitation, recognizing the qualities and areas where you need to improve.

This self-awareness allows you to take calculated risks and make informed decisions that align with your vision as an entrepreneur.

Monetizing on your strengths and weaknesses becomes imperative at this stage. You understand that making money is not the ultimate goal but rather the ability to sustain wealth over a prolonged period. Thankfully, you possess the knowledge and expertise to generate income, but now, you are focused on the art of preserving and multiplying it. This pursuit is what some may refer to as generational wealth.

Generational wealth goes beyond the idea of accumulating riches within a lifetime. It encompasses creating a legacy, ensuring that the resources you have amassed will suffice not only for your lifetime but for the next generation as well. To achieve this, you must adopt a comprehensive approach that combines financial intelligence, astute investments, and a long-term vision.

One of the crucial steps to securing generational wealth is diversification. By investing in different sectors and assets, you reduce the risk of losing your wealth in the face of economic volatility. Financial education and constantly expanding your knowledge become essential in this journey. Embracing new technologies, understanding market trends, and staying ahead of the curve allows you to adapt and thrive even in rapidly changing environments.

In addition, creating a sustainable business model that generates consistent cash flow is vital. Instead of relying solely on one source of income, consider exploring multiple revenue streams that align with your skills and interests. This not only ensures the stability of your wealth but also provides opportunities for growth and expansion.

Moreover, philanthropy plays a significant role in the creation and preservation of generational wealth. By giving back to society and making a positive impact on your community, you not only contribute to the betterment of others but also forge enduring connections and networks. These connections can open doors to new opportunities and avenues of growth, benefiting both your personal and professional life.

Expanding your business empire while nurturing relationships and fostering a prosperous legacy requires unwavering dedication, perseverance, and adaptability. This moment of complete solitude grants you the clarity to reflect on your journey and identify the path forward. Embrace this auspicious moment, as you have conquered the lows and revelled in the highs - and chart a course that will continue to propel you towards the pinnacle of everlasting success.

***

"How am I supposed to get these orders out if you close your factory? What do you expect me to do with such short notice?". The financial pressures of the lockdown proved difficult for the factory owners, and shortly after the world opened up, they closed down, leaving me and my brand perplexed on how to proceed from once again, another setback.
"Sorry Miss, we will see what we can do".
I never heard back from them after that phone call, as they filed bankruptcy and disappeared.
I was forced to get my thinking cap on to determine the best route possible for the survival of my brand. *There is no way that it can fall only months after starting up,* I thought. I refused to take defeat as an answer, so immediately found a way around this whole situation.

Sleepless nights found me again, whilst a high coffee intake became my closest bond. And there I searched high and low for manufacturers to take over last minute. The entrepreneurial spirit never left me, if anything, it allowed me to navigate through this stressful period ironically without, stress. I knew from past experiences that everything has a solution, it's just how willing I was to make those solutions work.

Knowing I had a limited amount of time, I attempted, and eventually succeeded in 'manufacturing' these products myself. With research, time, and dedication, it was possible. I knew I had to do this as a last-minute resort to rectify the situation as calmly as I knew how.

It was not an easy task, as I had to learn the intricate details of manufacturing and ensure that the quality of my products remained impeccable. I immersed myself in books, online tutorials, and attended workshops to gain as much knowledge as possible. I reached out to industry experts for advice and sought guidance from experienced entrepreneurs who had faced similar challenges.

The process of manufacturing my own products was arduous and required an immense amount of effort. I had to source the necessary materials, set up a production line, hire and train a small remote team, and manage the entire manufacturing process. It was a steep learning curve, but one that I embraced wholeheartedly.

Throughout this process, I realized the importance of resilience and adaptability. I had to quickly adapt to unforeseen circumstances and find alternative solutions when faced with setbacks. Flexibility became my mantra, as I learned to pivot and adjust my plans to meet the demands of the situation.

Patience played a crucial role as well. Building a manufacturing setup from scratch is time-consuming and requires meticulous attention to detail. I had to remain patient during the initial stages when progress seemed slow, trusting that each step was bringing me closer to my goal.

While the challenges were numerous, I also discovered hidden opportunities along the way. By taking on the manufacturing process myself, I gained a deeper understanding of my products and was able to make improvements and customizations that I had previously relied on external manufacturers for. This allowed me to create a unique selling point for my brand and differentiate myself in the market.

The experience of facing and overcoming these challenges strengthened my confidence as an entrepreneur. It reminded me of my ability to solve problems, make tough decisions, and persevere in the face of adversity. It further solidified my belief in my brand's potential and instilled in me a relentless determination to succeed.

As months went by and my brand started gaining traction, I realized that these challenges had become stepping stones, propelling me forward instead of holding me back. I learned that setbacks and obstacles are not roadblocks, but rather opportunities for growth and self-improvement.

Looking back, I am grateful for the challenges I faced during that difficult period. They forced me to think creatively, to push myself out of my comfort zone, and to rely on my strengths and knowledge. I emerged from that experience stronger and more resilient, with a brand that was not only surviving but thriving.

Of course, challenges presented itself here and there, but luckily with the experiences I had previously learned from, there was no room for serious error. Challenges are an inevitable part of any entrepreneurial journey. However, it is how we respond to these challenges that ultimately determines our success. By drawing on past experiences and adopting a determined mindset, I was able to navigate through the hurdles and find creative solutions. The setbacks I faced only served to strengthen my resolve and reinforce the unwavering belief I have in my brand's potential.

# FAITH

Faith is an integral part of our lives. It provides us with a sense of purpose, guidance, and strength to navigate through the wizardry of life. Without faith, we are left feeling lost, uncertain, and vulnerable. It is our belief in something greater than ourselves that keeps us grounded and helps us make difficult decisions with clarity and conviction.

For me, faith in God has played a significant role in shaping my character and providing direction in my life. As I reflect on the years prior, I can clearly see how God's goodness had guided me through the chaos and uncertainties I faced. It was through my faith in God that I was able to discover my true gifts and talents.

When I felt lost and didn't know where to turn, it was through prayer and reflection that I found the direction I needed. God's wisdom and guidance helped me channel my energy towards meaningful pursuits. Instead of succumbing to the pressures and distractions of the world, I focused my efforts on things that truly mattered.
It was also the faith instilled in me that summoned courage and fearlessness, to continuously push myself outside my comfort zone.

It is only when we step out of our comfort zone that we truly grow and reach our full potential. With God by my side, I felt a sense of assurance and strength to overcome any obstacles that stood in my way.

It was equally my faith in God that motivated me to give back to those less fortunate. It is through acts of kindness and generosity that we create a positive impact in the lives of others. When I had the means, I felt compelled to help those who were in need. God's love and compassion inspired me to extend a helping hand whenever possible.

In moments of confusion, stress, joy, and disbelief, turning to my faith became a vital point of call. It provided me with solace and reassurance during challenging times and allowed me to experience humility during moments of joy. Faith acted as an anchor, keeping me grounded and preventing me from making rash and irrational choices.

Life is full of risks and uncertainties. Without a foundation of faith, it becomes easy to make hasty decisions driven by fear or impulsiveness. Faith enables us to make decisions with a clear mind and a calm heart, knowing that there is a purpose and plan for our lives. It is crucial to have faith in something meaningful to us, as it acts as a compass, pointing us in the right direction on journeys we create for the betterment of our lives.

The power of prayer is a universal phenomenon that transcends religious affiliations and beliefs. It is an act that allows us to connect with a higher power, to seek solace, guidance, and ultimately find peace within ourselves. Prayer has the ability to transform our lives, providing us with a sense of hope, comfort, and strength during times of adversity. This personal experience of mine serves as a testament to the transformative power of prayer.

\*\*\*

The backdrop of this experience proved to be a challenging time in my life, a period marked by financial turmoil and deep uncertainty. The bankruptcy of the factory that manufactured my brand's products had left me in a state of confusion, as I grappled with the harsh realities of the aftermath. Determined to rectify the financial implications it had left me with, in a constant back and forth with the bank, I had spent the entire night immersed in a frustrating cycle of disputing. Exhausted mentally and emotionally, I yearned for respite from the overwhelming burden that had enveloped me.

In that moment, as I leaned back in my chair, I made a conscious decision to seek solace in prayer. Closing my eyes, I allowed myself to be vulnerable, addressing my concerns directly to a higher power. There was a profound sense of surrender, as I relinquished control and entrusted my struggles to God. This act of prayer was not merely a recitation of words, but a genuine plea for guidance, strength, and a revelation to show me the right path.

"Heavenly Father, it is you that has done this for me, it is also you that can take this away from me. If this is the direction I am supposed to take, if this is your will, Lord I ask for your guidance. Guide me when I am derailing and give me the faith to come to you when I need a revelation. Heavenly Father, I thank you, I love you and I am pleading for your mercy".

As I opened my eyes, I felt a significant weight lift off my shoulders. It was as if the burdens that had encapsulated me had been replaced with a renewed sense of hope and clarity.

Prayer allowed me to distance myself from the noise and negativity that had been consuming my thoughts, and instead, focus on developing a deep connection with something greater than myself. In that moment, it became abundantly clear that all that mattered was my relationship with God and His guidance.

The beauty of prayer lies in its ability to transcend the tangible aspects of life. It is not confined to a specific religion, doctrine, or dogma. Instead, it serves as a profound tool for personal introspection and spiritual growth. It provides us with an opportunity to lay bare our fears, hopes, and aspirations, allowing us to find solace and strength in the face of adversity. This experience revealed to me the importance of incorporating prayer into my daily routine, a consistent practice that would enable me to navigate the challenges that life presents with unwavering faith.

This encounter with prayer served as a reminder of the boundless love and support that God bestows upon us. It reminded me that His guidance is always accessible, that He is ever present, patiently waiting for us to seek His assistance. The act of prayer not only facilitated the resolution of my financial predicament but also aided in fostering a deeper connection with my faith, serving as a source of strength and comfort in all aspects of my life.

# BODY

We get so caught up in our work, responsibilities, and obligations that we often neglect one of the most important aspect of our lives - our physical health and appearance. We become so focused on achieving our goals and meeting deadlines that we forget to take care of ourselves.

Neglecting our physical health can have serious consequences. Lack of sleep becomes a common occurrence as we work late into the night, sacrificing our rest for the sake of productivity. This lack of sleep not only leaves us feeling tired and drained, but it also weakens our immune system. With a weakened immune system, we become more prone to illnesses and infections, making us even less productive in the long run.

A sedentary lifestyle and neglect of exercise leads to a decline in our physical fitness. Simple tasks, such as climbing a flight of stairs, become a challenge as we find ourselves out of breath and exhausted. Our bodies become unfit, causing us to gain weight and lose muscle tone. Suddenly, we find ourselves struggling to fit into our clothes, having to buy larger sizes to accommodate our expanding waistlines.

In addition to neglecting our physical fitness, we also disregard our appearance. We fail to invest time in grooming ourselves properly, resulting in dishevelled appearances and an overall lack of self-confidence. We may neglect regular haircuts or styling, forgetting to take care of our skin, or avoiding wearing clothes that make us feel good about ourselves. This neglect of our outer appearance can have a significant impact on our overall self-esteem and how we present ourselves to the world.

One of the main reasons for neglecting our physical health and appearance is the constant busyness of our lives. We live in a fast-paced world where time seems to slip away uncontrollably. We prioritize our work, studies, and other commitments, often at the expense of our own well-being. We forget that taking care of ourselves is not a luxury, but a necessity. Without good health, we cannot truly enjoy the fruits of our labour or achieve success in the long run.

To break free from this cycle of neglect, we must make a conscious effort to prioritize our physical health and appearance. We need to incorporate regular exercise into our daily routines, even if it means starting with small, manageable steps. Taking short breaks from work to stretch or go for a walk can do wonders for our physical well-being.

Paying attention to our diet is crucial. Being able to nourish our bodies with nutritious food, and drink plenty of water to stay hydrated is pivotal to good health. Avoiding excessive caffeine and sugar intake, such as that found in our favourite sodas, is essential for maintaining energy levels and overall health. It is important to listen to what our bodies truly need, rather than succumbing to unhealthy cravings.

Be careful to not underestimate the power of self-care and self-presentation. Allocating time for grooming, skincare, and dressing well can significantly boost our confidence and overall sense of self-worth. Taking pride in our appearance is not a vain pursuit but a reflection of the love and care we have for ourselves. By making small changes and consciously taking care of our bodies, we can improve our overall physical health and appearance, ultimately leading to a more fulfilling and successful life.

***

As I entered the makeup store, I couldn't help but get lost in the mesmerizing display of vibrant colours and enticing aromas. The shelves were lined with countless options, each product promising to enhance my beauty and leaving me scented like a bed of roses.

With my hands full of shopping bags with pre-bought sports apparel, I found myself contemplating whether I needed any more makeup. After all, my primary goal was to get back into shape and improve my fitness routine. However, an inner voice reminded me of the importance of maintaining a social image, especially for someone aspiring to be the face of a brand.

The truth is, our appearance plays a significant role in how others perceive us, whether or not we like to admit it. I understood that the image I portrayed had a direct impact on my personal and professional win. So, as contradictory as it may seem, exploring that store had its own justifications.

Makeup, for instance, has the power to transform and enhance our features, allowing us to present ourselves in the best possible light.

It can boost our self-esteem, giving us the confidence we need to conquer any challenge that comes our way. Whether it's a bold red lip, a flawless foundation, or a shimmering eye shadow, makeup enables us to express ourselves and make a statement.

As I pondered this realization, I decided to browse through the diverse array of makeup options available in the store. I picked up a few essentials that would both enhance my everyday look without overpowering my features, and also completely transform me when I felt like being a diva. A natural-looking foundation, a versatile mascara, and multiple lipstick shades were among my choices. Each product was carefully selected to create a polished appearance that would effortlessly transition from a day running errands to an evening of social events.

Leaving the store after a successful shopping spree, I couldn't help but be drawn towards the vibrant display of another boutique just a few steps away. The storefront exuded an air of elegance and sophistication, with rows upon rows of glamorous high heels on dazzling display. Intrigued by the promise of stepping into a world of heightened fashion, I decided to explore further.

You see, the femininity of dressing up has always held a special place in my heart. There is an indescribable joy that accompanies the act of adorning oneself in exquisite garments, not just for the sake of appearance, but also for the way it makes one feel. Glamour and luxury have a transformative effect, opening up a realm of fearlessness within us. It's as if, by donning these opulent ensembles, we are transported into a world where anything and everything feels possible.

Enthralled by the open invitation to explore this world, I found myself irresistibly drawn to the assortment of high heels that awaited me inside. As I drew closer, the sheer variety and craftsmanship of the footwear left me in awe. Each pair seemed to have its own personality, beckoning me to try them on and experience the magic they had to offer.

Among the many options before me, a few pairs instantly caught my eye. With detailed designs and bold colours, there was no way I was leaving without a pair... or two. Yet, it was a pair of patent black court heels that truly captured my heart. There was an understated elegance about them, a timeless allure that seemed to transcend trends and seasons.

Without hesitation, I slipped off my current shoes and delicately placed my feet into these sumptuous heels. Instantly, I felt a surge of confidence surge through my veins, as though I was imbued with a newfound grace and poise. The arch support provided by these magnificent shoes was unparalleled, giving me a sense of stability and comfort that enhanced my stride. As I walked around the store, their sleek design seemed to accentuate every step, transforming my attire into a work of art that resonated with glamour and finesse.

In that moment, I knew that these shoes were meant for me. They embodied everything I cherished - the embodiment of classic style and timeless taste. Their allure was not dependent on fleeting trends or passing fads; rather, they exuded a sense of enduring beauty that showcased my inherent elegance.

With conviction in my heart and a newfound spring in my step, I made my way to the counter, eager to make these heels my own. The minute I handed over my payment, I could feel a sense of satisfaction wash over me, knowing that this purchase would not just be a fashionable addition to my wardrobe, but a transformative investment in myself.

# TREPIDATION

Fear is an incredibly powerful emotion that can grip anyone, regardless of their position or circumstances. However, when it comes to business, fear can be particularly debilitating. It can seep into every aspect of an entrepreneur's life and hinder their ability to make rational decisions. In fact, many successful business owners admit that the worst feeling they have experienced throughout their journey is fear, especially after the initial struggle phase.

One phenomenon that often contributes to this fear is known as the imposter syndrome. This psychological pattern makes individuals doubt their abilities and accomplishments, leading them to believe that they are undeserving of their success. Despite evidence to the contrary, these individuals feel like frauds and fear that someone will eventually unveil their incompetence. This sense of unworthiness creates a perpetual state of anxiety, even when all external indicators suggest that they are thriving.

The imposter syndrome can be especially prevalent in the realm of business, where competition is fierce, and the stakes are high.

Entrepreneurs constantly compare themselves to their peers, scrutinizing their achievements with a critical eye. The fear of being exposed as a fraud drives them to work tirelessly, often sacrificing their mental well-being and personal lives in the process. This fear becomes a crushing weight on their shoulders, impeding their ability to celebrate their accomplishments and hindering their growth.

The fear experienced during the post-struggle phase of a business is magnified by the constant uncertainty of the entrepreneurial journey. In the early stages of any venture, there are numerous obstacles and challenges to overcome. Whether it's securing funding, attracting customers, or building a team, the path to success is fraught with setbacks and failures. Emerging from this initial struggle is a significant milestone, but it also brings about a new set of anxieties.

Entrepreneurs often fear that something will suddenly go wrong and obliterate all their hard work. They worry about losing clients, facing financial difficulties, or encountering unforeseen competition. This fear stems from the understanding that business triumph is not a linear trajectory, but rather a rollercoaster ride filled with unpredictable twists and turns. The fear of failure cripples their decision-making abilities, often leading them to play it safe rather than taking calculated risks that could potentially elevate their businesses to new heights.

Yet, despite the debilitating effects of fear, you must learn to acknowledge and conquer it. One way to combat these fears is through self-reflection and recognition of your achievements and capabilities.

Entrepreneurs need to remind themselves of their unique skills and experiences that have allowed them to build their businesses in the first place. They must embrace the idea that their success is not accidental but is a result of their hard work and dedication.

Additionally, seeking support from fellow entrepreneurs, mentors, or even joining networking groups can provide a sense of community and reassurance. Knowing that others have faced similar fears and have overcome them can be an immense source of hope and encouragement. Sharing experiences, seeking advice, and collaborating with others can help alleviate the imposter syndrome, create a support network, and instil a sense of confidence within entrepreneurs.

Fear is undoubtedly one of the worst feelings to experience during any phase of a journey. The perennial uncertainty of the company's direction can create a constant state of anxiety and hinder personal and professional growth; but by recognizing your capabilities, you can conquer these fears with one foot in front of the other.

***

As the alarm buzzed persistently, I jumped out of bed in a panic, realizing that it was already six o'clock in the morning. With the year coming to an end, I couldn't help the anticipation for what 2022 had in store for me. However, being jolted awake at such an early hour left me in a dazed and sleepy state, forcing my mind to struggle between the realms of dreams and reality.

As I rubbed the sleep out of my eyes, a wave of euphoria washed over me, filling my mind with thoughts of the upcoming evening.

I was invited to a dinner by a networking contact I had recently conversed with at an online webinar. It had only been a few weeks since that encounter, but the connection we formed had allowed me the honour of being invited to this exclusive gathering. The host had meticulously chosen fifteen individuals to attend the dinner, making me feel a sense of privilege and importance. The invitation had arrived a few days ago, detailing the time, location, and dress code for the event.

Now, standing in front of my wardrobe, I found myself contemplating between two dresses – a beautiful black one or an elegant blue one. Each dress held its own allure, promising to enhance my presence and leave a lasting impression on the other guests. It was a decision I had to make wisely, as the right attire could be a subtle reflection of my personality and professionalism.

With the dinner being an intimate affair, mingling with a select group of elite professionals, the pressure to make a favourable impression was palpable. This distinct gathering was an opportunity to forge new connections, exchange ideas, and potentially propel my career forward. The carefully curated guest list meant that each person present had something unique to bring to the table, both literally and figuratively.

Uniting individuals from diverse backgrounds, the evening promised to ignite intellectual curiosity and foster a sense of camaraderie. With only fifteen individuals in attendance, the intimate setting would encourage open dialogue and the exchange of valuable insights.

***

After freshening up for the day and nourishing my body with a hearty bowl of porridge, I fired up my laptop and began assessing the sales that were made during the night. My Executive Assistant, Selena, remotely working with me from the comfort of her home in Italy, handled the sales whilst I was asleep, and enthusiastically pinged over a new marketing pitch that would prove helpful for the end of year festivities. We chatted back and forth online for the greater part of the morning, doing and redoing the plan and going over the budget needed, with me eventually giving the final go ahead to make it happen.

It was chilly at midday, the birds isolated in the trees, passers-by wrapped up fit for the season. Focused on the gym in the distance, I found myself jogging towards it for the last two minutes there.
Not long after, I couldn't help but feel a tightening feeling in my chest whilst running. At first, I thought I was straining my body too much, but upon realizing I had only been on my feet for a few minutes, I froze and reacted observantly to the panic.
It didn't make sense for me to have felt that way - given my relatively well-trained lungs. Then it dawned on me that the uneasiness stemmed from a mental strain.
An insecurity.

For the first time in a long time, it was undeniable; I had a healthy amount of control in both my personal and professional life, to the extent of getting invited to exclusive dinners. Was I worthy of attending such?

I felt a sense of guilt. Guilt, that for the first time in a long time, my daily routine was smoother, I was happier, and most importantly, business couldn't be better.

It took me a few hard minutes, but I had to realize in that moment that I was deserving of everything that was happening in my life. I worked hard every single day, used my personal income to sustain the companies, and went through hell just to get to where I was.
It wasn't the money I was making that made me feel strange. It was the peace. I wasn't used to it.

What I worked for, the network I built, didn't happen overnight. It was a result of years of hard work, dedication, and uncompromisable battles. I had made sacrifices in my personal life, missing family gatherings and important events to focus on my business. I had made sacrifices in my professional life, taking on extra responsibilities and working long hours to ensure the success of my endeavours. But in the end, it was all worth it.

As I entered the gym and made my way to the weights, the feeling of strength and empowerment washed over me. Not just physical strength, but mental clarity as well. The ability to handle any challenge that comes my way with grace and resilience. The ability to weather any storm and come out stronger on the other side.

\*\*\*

As the hours ticked by and the evening approached, I put on my chosen dress, the blue one, and added the final touches to my appearance. I looked in the mirror and smiled, proud of the person I had become. I was no longer the timid and unsure person I once was in 2016. I had grown into a confident and self-assured individual, ready to take on whatever the future had in store for me.

As I walked into the restaurant for the dinner, I was greeted by the host with warmth and enthusiasm. The room was filled with young, successful individuals from various industries, all with their own stories of triumph and resilience. We shared stories, exchanged ideas, and celebrated our accomplishments. It was a night of camaraderie and inspiration, a reminder that success is not an isolated event, but a collective effort.

As the clock struck midnight and the year 2022 was ushered in with cheers and laughter, I couldn't help but feel a sense of gratitude. Gratitude for the opportunities that had come my way, gratitude for the people who had supported me throughout my journey, and gratitude for the peace and fulfilment I found in my life.

The year ahead was uncertain, filled with new challenges and opportunities. But with the peace I had found within myself, I knew that I was equipped to handle whatever came my way. I was ready to embrace the future with open arms, knowing that I deserved the happiness and success that awaited me.

And as I stepped into the new year, I vowed to continue striving for success while cherishing the peace that could sporadically come with it.

# DISORDER

As we journey towards our true calling, we often encounter a peculiar phenomenon: the presence of imitation fuelled by envy. As we begin to embrace our potential and actively pursue it, we may find ourselves surrounded by individuals who seemingly admire and want to emulate our every move. Instead of celebrating our accomplishments and encouraging us, these individuals may bring forth distraction and disorder, attempting to hinder us from reaching our full potential.

It is only natural for others to be drawn to those who have embraced their calling and are actively manifesting it in their lives. When we tap into our true potential, we radiate an energy that is magnetic, inspiring and captivating to others. As our actions reflect our purpose, we become beacons of hope and motivation to those around us. Thus, it's no surprise that many individuals gravitate towards us, hoping to absorb and replicate our chosen path.

However, not everyone's intentions are pure. Some people may approach us driven by envy, their admiration merely masking their own insecurities. These individuals may lack the courage or determination to pursue their own true calling.

Instead, they choose to mimic our actions, hoping that by doing so, they can taste a small fraction of our success. Yet, their intentions are not aligned with personal growth or the pursuit of their own passions; instead, they seek shortcuts and quick fixes.

Rather than fostering genuine celebration and support for our accomplishments, these imitators bring disorder into our lives. Their envy can lead them to engage in negative behaviours, such as spreading rumours, questioning our methods, or even deliberately hindering our progress. By doing so, they aim to blind us from reaching our full potential, out of fear that our success will only highlight their own shortcomings.

As we navigate the challenges presented by envious imitators, we can strengthen our resolve and focus on our own journey. By remaining steadfast in our pursuit of our true calling, we will continue to inspire and motivate individuals who are genuinely searching for their own path.

With that being said, it is important to cultivate a sense of empathy and understanding towards these imitators. While their actions may be misguided and fuelled by envy, it is crucial to remember that they, too, are on their own individual journeys. By showing compassion and empathy towards them, we may have the opportunity to inspire them to introspect and uncover their true potential, just as we have done for ourselves.

*\*\*\**

As I reflect upon my past, I realize that the once seemingly large and vibrant friendship group I belonged to had slowly dwindled in size.

Whether intentionally or unintentionally, my circle of friends has diminished over time; but what struck me the most is the discovery that one individual, whom I considered to be a great friend, had been sabotaging me behind my back.

It was a gradual revelation, and I found myself closely observing their actions and behaviour. The more I observed, the clearer it became that this supposed friend was actively working against me, attempting to defame my character and undermine my achievements. Although initially shocked and hurt by their actions, it was empowering to know that I was not oblivious to their motives and had the wisdom to recognize their true nature.

Deciding not to confront this friend was not an easy choice. Confrontations require significant time and energy, something I did not possess at that moment. Besides, I knew that their guilt would eat at them, and they would eventually distance themselves from me. And that's precisely what happened. Their subconscious realization of their betrayal led them to withdraw from our friendship, creating a natural distance between us.

From that moment on, I became more vigilant. I understood that even your closest friends can unexpectedly turn into your truest enemies, cunningly plotting your ultimate downfall. It was disheartening to realize that someone I considered trustworthy could harbour such deception.

As much as the betrayal and subsequent loss of friends were significant hurdles to overcome, I also discovered another disheartening truth.

Men who lacked personal security and self-confidence were particularly intimated by not only my achievements but also by my mere presence as a strong and independent woman. It was as if my self-assured demeanour acted as a force that made them question their own abilities and worth.

This realization brought forth mixed emotions within me. On one hand, I felt a sense of sadness that society's perception of masculinity had led some individuals to feel threatened by strong women. On the other hand, it generated a greater determination to continue being myself, unabashedly embracing my achievements and empowering others to do the same.

# BALANCE

On occasion, it may seem like there is no time to take a break. The demands of running a business, especially in the initial stages, can feel overwhelming. However, just like any other employee, taking time off is crucial in order to avoid burnout and maintain a healthy work-life balance.

Burnout is a real danger for both entrepreneurs and employees. It is a state of physical, emotional, and mental exhaustion caused by prolonged periods of stress and overwork. Entrepreneurs often think that they can push through and continue working without breaks, as they are driven by their passion and the desire to succeed. This approach is dangerous and can lead to detrimental effects on their well-being, and ultimately on the success of their business.

Taking time off is not a sign of weakness or laziness, but rather a necessary means of recharging and rejuvenating. Just as employees need vacation time to relax and escape from the daily grind, entrepreneurs need time to rest and recharge their batteries as well. This time away from work allows them to gain perspective, reflect on their goals, and come back with renewed energy and creativity.

While there may be differences in the way entrepreneurs and employees take time off, the reasons behind it remain the same. Whether it is a day off, a weekend getaway, a longer vacation, or even a month of doing nothing, the purpose is to disconnect from work and focus on personal interests, hobbies, and relationships. This precious time spent away from work allows individuals to nurture their personal well-being, strengthen relationships, and find inspiration outside of their business.

Taking time off can also have a positive impact on the business itself. Stepping away from the day-to-day operations allows entrepreneurs to delegate tasks and empower their employees to take on more responsibility. This not only helps to develop and empower their team, but also allows the entrepreneur to focus on the bigger picture and long-term strategy of the business.

It is crucial for entrepreneurs to recognize that taking time off does not equate to negligence or a lack of commitment. In fact, it is an essential part of being a successful entrepreneur.

***

As the night lay over the horizon, casting darkness across my room, I awoke remembering the long British Airways flight that awaited me.
It wasn't long before I found myself on yet another visit to Kenya, a place that had captivated my heart on my previous visit. From the moment the idea of a vacation had entered my mind, my heart yearned for the serenity and tranquillity that only a break from the mundane can bring.

With a noticeable spring in my step, I carefully wheeled my suitcase through the airport, feeling the familiar sense of thrill as each step brought me closer to embarking on another adventure. The bustling airport terminal was alive with a mix of eager tourists, harried businessfolk, and families embarking on their own holiday getaways. It was a symphony of excited chatter, echoing through the air.

Usually, I would find myself at the flight's gate helplessly waiting to board, impatiently shifting my weight from one foot to another in hopes of speeding up time. However, this time I decided to veer away from my established routine and treated myself to a wholesome breakfast at the airport.

As I settled myself in a cosy corner of a restaurant, the aroma of freshly brewed coffee and the melodious rattle of clinking cutlery enveloped my senses, setting the perfect pre-holiday mood.

Savouring every sip of rich, dark coffee and relishing the taste of a freshly baked croissant, I allowed myself to ease into the moment, embracing the anticipation of what lay ahead. The gentle hum of conversations around me blended harmoniously with the background music, creating a soothing ambiance that melted away any remnants of stress or worry from my mind. It was in these moments of mindful indulgence that I found solace and a true sense of being present.

As I watched the world around me, I couldn't help but appreciate the diversity of travellers passing through the airport. Each person carried their own stories, their own dreams, and desires. The airport, in its bustling glory, became a microcosm of humanity, reminding me of the vastness of the world and the endless possibilities it held.

And as I observed the people bustling and the planes soaring overhead, I graciously awaited my turn.

Fuelled by this gratitude and the breakfast that had nourished my body and soul, I emerged from the café rejuvenated and ready to immerse myself in the magic that awaited in Kenya. The airport, once a mere transit point, had become an integral part of my journey, a place where I could savour the anticipation and appreciate the beauty of my chosen destination.

In hindsight, that wholesome breakfast at the airport acted as a catalyst for my overall holiday experience. It reminded me to slow down and savour the journey, not just the destination. It taught me that sometimes, taking a moment to indulge in the simple pleasures of life can have a profound impact on our overall well-being.

So, as I stepped onto the plane, the engines roaring to life beneath me, I carried with me a renewed sense of wonder and appreciation. Kenya awaited, promising adventures and memories yet to be made. And as the wheels lifted off the ground, I knew that this holiday would be a testament to the power of a simple breakfast, and the joy it could ignite within me.

As the plane began its descent almost nine hours later, a rush of angst washed over me. The turbulence that had plagued the entire flight intensified, turning my worst nightmare into a grim reality. I clenched the armrests, my knuckles turning white, as the aircraft shook uncontrollably. Dark clouds loomed ominously outside the small window, casting an eerie shadow over the plane. Bad weather had decided to grace us with its presence, as if mocking our desire for a smooth journey.

planned itinerary, I lay in bed that night with a wavering curiosity. I was unaware of what the next two weeks held in store for me, but I revelled in the thrill of the unknown.

As I closed my eyes, the comfort of the bed embraced me, cocooning me in a warm embrace that melted away any remaining traces of fatigue. The soft pillows, adorned with fresh linen, cradled my head, inviting me into a dream-filled slumber. I surrendered to the sweet release of sleep, knowing that in the morning, a world of new experiences would await me.

Vacations often hold the promise of exciting discoveries and memorable moments. They serve as an escape from the monotonous daily routine, offering a chance to unwind and explore unfamiliar territories. This trip was no different. It was an opportunity for me to detach from the familiarity of my everyday life and immerse myself in a vibrant, foreign culture.

The next two weeks unfolded like chapters in a fascinating novel. Each day presented unique experiences, from exploring the bustling streets of Nairobi to venturing into the breath-taking landscapes of nearby national parks. I indulged in local cuisine, engaging in conversations with friendly residents who were more than eager to share their stories and traditions. The apartment, my temporary haven, provided a cosy respite after days filled with adventure, offering me comfort and relaxation.

As the days passed, my appreciation for this slice of paradise grew. The spaciousness of the apartment allowed me to unwind and re-energize after long days of exploration, while its comforting ambiance created a sense of home away from home.

It became a sanctuary where I could reflect on the day's events and prepare mentally for the adventures that awaited me in the coming days.

Nairobi, the bustling capital of Kenya, was just the beginning of my East African adventure. As I embarked on my journey, I made an exhilarating decision to explore various countries within the East African continent. Little did I know that one city in particular would capture my heart and leave an indelible mark on my soul – Zanzibar, located in Tanzania.

From the moment I arrived in Zanzibar, I could sense a special aura, an energy that was distinct from any other place I had visited. The locals greeted me with warm smiles and open arms, instantly making me feel at home. Their hospitality was unparalleled, and their genuine friendliness put my mind at ease.

As I ventured through the narrow, winding streets of the famous Stone Town, an ancient trading hub that still holds remnants of its past, I felt a sense of calm overwhelm me. The architecture stood as a testament to a rich history, with Arab, Persian, Indian, and European influences blending together seamlessly. It was a true melting pot of cultures, and it fascinated me to see how different traditions coexisted.

Zanzibar is renowned for its pristine beaches, and I had the pleasure of strolling along the powdery white sands, with the turquoise Indian Ocean stretching out before me. The sight was nothing short of breath-taking. I couldn't resist dipping my toes into the crystal-clear waters, the gentle waves lapping against my skin. The beach became my sanctuary, a place where I could retreat from the world and immerse myself in the tranquil beauty of nature.

But it wasn't just the natural wonders that captivated me; the food in Zanzibar was a delightful revelation. The fusion of African, Arabian, and Indian flavours resulted in a culinary extravaganza. From freshly caught seafood to aromatic curries, my taste buds were constantly tantalized. The locals took pride in their cuisine, and their passion was evident in every bite. I savoured the moment, proud of the rich tapestry of flavours that encapsulated my African heritage.

In Zanzibar, time seemed to slow down, allowing me to reflect and appreciate the simple joys in life. Boat trips to nearby islands revealed hidden gems, from vibrant coral reefs teeming with marine life to the awe-inspiring sight of dolphins dancing in the open sea. The serenity of the moment was overwhelming, reminding me of the power of nature and the profound bond we share with the world around us.

As I concluded my journey through the East African cities, Zanzibar remained etched in my memory. It was a place that taught me the power of genuine human connection, the beauty of cultural diversity, and the importance of appreciating the natural wonders that surround us. Zanzibar had become my favourite stop, a testament to the profound love I hold for my African heritage.

Arriving back in the UK, after a much-needed holiday, was like a breath of fresh air. Although there was a tinge of sadness that the vacation had come to an end, the feeling of being revitalized and renewed overwhelmed me. The weight of work burnout had been lifted, and I found myself beaming from ear to ear, radiating an undeniable glow of determination. This getaway had served its purpose and had given me the necessary rejuvenation to tackle any pressure tailgating me.

More than just a superficial physical transformation, the holiday had expanded my mind and broadened my horizons. Through immersing myself in new cultures, tasting exotic cuisines, and exploring unfamiliar landscapes, my travels had nurtured my curiosity and ignited my creative spark. This newfound perspective had shown me the first things I needed to work on to elevate my brand to where I truly wanted it to be.

One of the key realizations during my journey was the importance of authenticity. It became evident that in order to stand out in a crowded marketplace, I needed to stay true to myself and my values. The holiday had allowed me to detach from the noise and demands of work, affording me the clarity to identify the unique elements that set me apart. Armed with this knowledge, I was ready to inject my personal touch into every aspect of my brand, making it genuinely representative of who I am and what I stand for.

It was mostly the exposure to different cultures had taught me the power of adaptability. Witnessing various approaches and strategies employed by businesses in foreign countries, I recognized the need to remain flexible and open-minded in today's fast-paced world. This was instantly reflected as I returned to the UK. I became determined to be more adaptable in my own business practices, ready to embrace change and quickly respond to new trends or challenges that would come my way.

The holiday also rekindled my passion for innovation and creativity. Experiencing cultures and ideas different from my own sparked a fire within me, encouraging me to think beyond the conventional and push the boundaries of my own abilities. It reminded me that growth and progress -

cannot be achieved by staying within comfort zones but rather by continuously exploring new territories and ideas. Armed with this mindset, I felt motivated and inspired to take risks and explore innovative strategies that would elevate my brand to new heights.

This was not just a mere vacation; it was an opportunity to immerse myself in new cultures and ideas. Little did I know that this experience would ignite a passion within me, a passion for innovation that had been lying dormant for far too long. It was a journey that would challenge me to think beyond the conventional, to push the boundaries of my abilities, and to dare to dream big.

As I ventured into foreign lands, I was welcomed by a kaleidoscope of sights, sounds, and tastes. Each encounter with a different culture brought with it a fresh perspective and a wealth of new ideas. I found myself captivated by the diversity, eager to learn and absorb as much as I could. From the bustling streets of Juba to the ancient ruins of Rome, every destination unveiled a unique facet of human creativity. It was as though I had stumbled upon a treasure trove of inspiration.

The holiday served as a powerful reminder that growth and progress cannot be achieved by simply staying within our comfort zones. It is through venturing into new territories and embracing the unfamiliar that we truly expand our horizons. This realization pushed me to step out of the safety net of my routine and challenge myself in ways I had never thought possible.

Armed with this mindset, I was enamoured with genuine inspiration. I was no longer content with mediocrity; but yearned to take risks and explore innovative strategies that would elevate my brand to new heights.

# DISPARITY

Friendships and relationships are complex concepts that vary from person to person. They are built on different foundations, and they evolve over time as individuals change and grow; but there are certain aspects that can help us define these connections and understand the dynamics that occur when two minds drift apart.

Friendship can be defined as a deep bond between two individuals who share mutual trust, understanding, and support. It is characterized by a sense of loyalty, companionship, and shared experiences. Friends are often seen as an extension of ourselves, someone with whom we can be our authentic selves. They provide emotional support, offer different perspectives, and celebrate our achievements. While friendship can sometimes be spontaneous, it requires effort, investment, and a genuine connection from both parties to thrive.

On the other hand, relationships encompass a broader spectrum, including friendships, romantic partnerships, family ties, and professional connections. These relationships are interconnected by bonds formed through various contexts and shared understanding.

Relationships are more encompassing and often involve a deeper level of commitment and interdependence.

When two minds start to drift apart, it can be a natural progression that occurs as individuals grow and change. People undergo personal transformations, acquiring new interests, beliefs, and priorities that may not align with their past companions. Such drifts can be gradual or sudden, and it can result from diverse factors such as geographical relocation, changes in life stages, or simply diverging interests and goals.

In some cases, this shift in interests and perspectives can introduce excitement into the relationship. The presence of contrasting viewpoints, hobbies, and passions can make interactions more stimulating and enriching. It enables individuals to learn from one another, challenge their preconceptions, and broaden their horizons. The saying "opposites attract" can hold some truth in these cases, as the diversity in interests can provide an opportunity for personal growth and expanding one's worldview. However, for this dynamic to be sustainable, both parties must be open-minded, respectful, and willing to find common ground despite their differences.

When two minds drift apart significantly, reaching a complete separation can become inevitable. It becomes increasingly challenging to maintain understanding and connection when fundamental values and interests no longer align. This disconnect can strain the relationship, leading to distance, conflicts, and eventual dissolution. It can be a painful and difficult realization when we find ourselves at odds with someone we once considered close. It may require honest conversations, emotional processing, and accepting that the relationship may have run its course.

As life is constantly changing, it is important to recognize that relationships will naturally evolve as well. It is crucial to communicate openly and honestly with those we care about, both in moments of cohesion and during times of drift. This allows for understanding, empathy, and the possibility of finding shared interests or compatible paths even when two minds appear to be heading in different directions.

*\*\**

"I don't think this is for me if I'm honest, I tried my best." These words echoed in my mind, lingering like a haunting melody. They were uttered by a friend, who was starting out in the catering side of business, recently launching their take on the trade one month prior. We had shared our life experiences, dreams, and aspirations, but now it seemed that our paths were diverging.

Back in 2016, I could have easily comprehended where my friend was coming from. We were young and naïve, expecting immediate success and gratification in our endeavours. But as the clock ticked closer to 2023, my perspective had changed, coloured by the vast knowledge I had accumulated over time. I understood that building a successful business was not an overnight feat; it required patience, perseverance, and resilience.

My friend seemed to lack this understanding, expecting reasonable profit right from the start. Perhaps they were influenced by the romanticized stories of overnight successes and viral sensations that saturated social media and popular culture. But the reality, as I had learned, was much different. It can take years, even up to five in some extreme cases, to see a breakthrough in business.

It was disheartening to realize that our conversations had become difficult, even strained. We were mentally inhabiting two different worlds. While I had grown accustomed to the long and arduous journey within this line of work, my friend appeared to be stuck in the illusion of instant gratification. Our paths had clashed, and our perspectives on life and success had diverged with them.

I was no longer able to share my struggles, my setbacks, and my triumphs with this person. They had become disconnected from the reality of building something meaningful, both professionally and personally. While I understood their frustration, it saddened me to witness their impatience and lack of perseverance.

It is an unfortunate reality that as we grow older, our interests and priorities often shift. It is a natural part of the human experience, but that doesn't make it any less heart-breaking when it happens to friendships. Witnessing the changes in interests as friends grow into adults can be a truly unfair and confusing experience.

There is a certain beauty in the idea of friends growing together, supporting each other, and celebrating each other's victories. We often imagine a future where we and our friends achieve success, happiness, and fulfilment together. We envision a bond that withstands the test of time, one that grows stronger as we all navigate the complexities of adulthood. However, life rarely unfolds according to our plans, and sometimes our friends simply do not have the same zeal or ambition to carry through.

As time passed, it became evident that our conversations began to lack the vigour and intellect that once defined them.

What used to be thought-provoking discussions about dreams, aspirations, and the world around us slowly transform into mundane chats about trivial matters. It is disheartening to see the passion and excitement we shared fade away, replaced by shallow exchanges that fail to stimulate our minds or emotions.

This shift in interests and conversations often leaves us torn. On the one hand, we recognize that we shouldn't be heartless and distance ourselves from our friends simply because our conversations and interests no longer align. After all, friendships should be based on unconditional support and understanding. It feels wrong to abandon these relationships that have brought us comfort and companionship for so long.

On the other hand, we yearn for connections with people who not only understand but share our current interests and passions. We crave conversations that ignite our intellect, challenge our perspectives, and drive us to grow as individuals. It is only natural to seek out companions who align with our evolving goals and desires, as this is essential to our personal growth and fulfilment.

In our contemporary society, where instant gratification is glorified and quick results are expected, it is vital for aspiring entrepreneurs and individuals to embrace a different mindset. Success is a marathon, not a sprint. It requires dedication, belief, and an unwavering commitment to one's goals. Rome wasn't built in a day, and neither is a successful business.

While it was difficult to accept that my friend could not comprehend the journey I was on, I had to recognize that we were simply at different stages of our lives. Our mentalities had evolved differently, shaped by -

diverse experiences and insights. And though it was painful to let go of that friendship, I knew that it was essential for my own growth and progress.

As I moved forward, continuing to navigate the intricate path of entrepreneurship, I sought out like-minded individuals who shared my vision and understood the trials and tribulations that come with it. Surrounding myself with those who believed in the long-term process, rather than immediate gains, has been instrumental in my personal and professional development.

So, despite the sting of hearing those challenging words from a friend, I realized that it was a pivotal moment in my journey. It served as a reminder that not everyone would understand or appreciate the sacrifices, the determination, and the patience required to build something substantial. But for those who do, the connections and friendships forged along the way would be invaluable.

In the end, I had to accept that our paths had diverged, and that was okay. I had evolved through my experiences, and now it was time to find others who shared my mindset. Business is not for the faint-hearted, but for those who are willing to endure and persist, the rewards can be immeasurable.

# SECLUSION

As individuals traverse through life, it is inevitable that their priorities will shift and change. What once held great importance in their younger years may now pale in comparison to what lies ahead. Similarly, as we mature, the size and significance of our friendships tend to diminish, while the prominence of jealousy begins to manifest itself more publicly. These changes are not necessarily negative; rather, they reflect the evolution and growth we experience along life's journey.

As children, our priorities are often centred around simple and immediate needs such as playtime, toys, and the desire for attention. However, as we navigate adolescence and eventually adulthood, our priorities naturally expand and diversify. Education, career aspirations, and personal development become paramount as we mature. We begin to recognize the importance of building a stable future, paving the way for success, and leaving a mark in our chosen fields. Thus, the focus shifts from momentary pleasures to long-term goals, ultimately driving our ambitions and shaping our lives.

The concept of friendship also undergoes transformation as we grow.

In our younger years, friendships seem boundless and limitless. We effortlessly form connections with classmates, neighbours, and even random strangers on the playground. In this youthful innocence, we lack the discernment and awareness to distinguish between genuine, lifelong friendships and transient acquaintances. As we mature, the circle of close friends tends to become smaller and more selective.

We learn to appreciate quality over quantity, recognizing the significance of trust, loyalty, and shared values. Moreover, as life responsibilities increase, time becomes a scarce resource, prompting us to invest it wisely in those relationships that truly nurture our growth and well-being.

One particularly striking change that becomes more evident as we grow is the evolving nature of envy. In our younger years, jealousy tends to simmer beneath the surface, kept predominantly within the confines of our hearts. As we age, however, social dynamics and external expectations force this jealousy to become more public. In an era dominated by social media, where highlight reels are presented while challenges and insecurities are often hidden, envy can flare up and manifest overtly. Comparison becomes a toxic habit, leading to gossip, rivalry, and a general sense of discontent. Nevertheless, with maturity comes the realization that jealousy serves no purpose other than to hinder our growth and happiness.

As we become more self-aware, we learn to celebrate others' successes and channel our energy towards self-improvement, acknowledging that everyone's journey is unique and personal achievements should be based on our own aspirations.

***

As life progressed, relationships changed, priorities shifted, and I found myself becoming more guarded and reserved. The naivety of my youth had been replaced with a cautiousness that stemmed from past disappointments and betrayals.

The eery silence in my bedroom every morning, in comparison to my once busy phone, seemed to amplify these thoughts and emotions. It whispered reminders of the fear of vulnerability. It was in that stillness that I realized the true weight of my own thoughts and the impact they had on my life.

In an attempt to combat the loneliness and longing, I turned to technology. The cloud-based app on my phone became a portal to the past, holding countless memories captured in photographs. I scrolled through them, reliving moments of laughter, adventures, and camaraderie. But as I lingered on a particular photo of my friends and I, I felt a pang of nostalgia and longing.

The image portrayed a carefree version of myself, surrounded by friends who were once an integral part of my life. We had spent hours at the mall, indulging in retail therapy, sharing inside jokes, and creating lasting memories. Looking at the smiles on our faces, I couldn't help but miss the social and vibrant person I used to be.

In that moment, it became clear to me that friendships are not easily forged, especially as you grow older. The world becomes filled with unauthentic people, those who are more interested in what they can gain from you rather than forming genuine connections. It's harder to discern who is truly a valuable asset in your life.

This realization made me yearn for the freedom I once had. The freedom to engage with others without fear of judgment or betrayal. But I also knew that I couldn't go back to the naivety of my early youth. Life had taught me the importance of discernment and self-preservation.

As the silence lingered in my room, I realized that I didn't have to succumb to the loneliness or remain a prisoner of my own thoughts. I could reclaim my social vibrancy while still maintaining a sense of caution. I could seek out those who proved themselves to be authentic and trustworthy, while being mindful of my own boundaries and self-care.

The eery silence had served its purpose. It reminded me of the value of companionship and connection, but also of the importance of self-awareness and protection. It was in that moment, immersed in the stillness, that I made a silent vow to myself - to seek out genuine friendships, to embrace vulnerability while staying true to who I had become, and to never settle for anything less than what I deserved.

As the morning unfolded and the night sky dissipated, I welcomed a new glimmer of hope. I knew that the road ahead wouldn't be easy, that there would be obstacles and disappointments along the way. But I also knew that I had the power to create the kind of friendships that would enrich my life, rather than deplete it.

# MINDSET

What we want, we can get, and we will get. It just depends on how badly we want it.
Now, what are *you* willing to sacrifice to ensure that you get it?

Sometimes we become so engrossed with the fact that many things are not within reach, or to some 'impossible'. Many things are not impossible; they just require sacrifice.

In life, we often encounter dreams, goals, and aspirations that sometimes seem out of reach. We look at others who have accomplished similar feats and wonder how they managed to attain their desired outcomes. We may think that they possess exceptional qualities or have been blessed with luck, disregarding the sacrifices and hard work they endured to accomplish their dreams.

Whether it be a personal ambition or a professional goal, obtaining what we desire demands a certain level of commitment and sacrifice. The truth is, no matter how badly we want something, it will remain elusive if we are not willing to make sacrifices to attain it.

Sacrifice often involves giving up certain things that are of lesser importance to us in order to achieve what we truly desire. It may entail sacrificing time, energy, comfort, or even relationships. Sacrifice requires dedication, grit, and perseverance. It demands that we prioritise our objectives and make conscious choices to allocate our resources effectively.

For instance, imagine a young entrepreneur who dreams of starting their own business. They may have an extraordinary idea, filled with potential, and are captivated by the prospect of achieving success in their chosen field. However, they soon realise that starting a business requires relentless effort, long hours, financial investments, and personal sacrifices. They may need to give up their social life, their comfort zone, and even financial security to pursue their entrepreneurial pursuits. Despite the difficulties, if the young entrepreneur is truly passionate about their vision, they will gladly embrace the necessary sacrifices, knowing that it will be worthwhile in the end.

Similarly, consider a person who dreams of becoming a professional athlete. They understand that achieving greatness in their chosen sport will necessitate years of intense training, rigorous physical conditioning, and an unwavering commitment to their craft. They may need to sacrifice their leisure time, prioritize strict diets and exercise regimens, and endure endless setbacks and failures. Only through perseverance and a willingness to forego momentary pleasures can they transform their dreams into reality.

While sacrifice serves as the catalyst for success, it is not a decision to be made lightly. Sacrifice entails leaving behind certain aspects of our lives that bring us joy and comfort.

It may involve distancing ourselves from toxic relationships, giving up material possessions, or even accepting temporary discomfort. However, it is important to remember that these sacrifices are not permanent; they are stepping stones towards a greater goal.

Recognizing the necessity of sacrifice instils a sense of purpose. When we are aware of the sacrifices required, we become more disciplined. We understand that the challenges we face are temporary and serve as stepping stones towards our ultimate objective. Sacrifice helps us develop resilience, as it requires us to push beyond our boundaries and confront our fears. It teaches us the value of perseverance and the gratifying feeling of achievement that comes from surmounting obstacles.

\*\*\*

South Kensington, an area that boasts luxury and substantial wealth, also holds a special place in my heart. As I walked around, I found myself marvelling at the grandeur and beauty that surrounded me. The lavish homes, designer boutiques, and elegant architecture truly painted a picture of opulence and prosperity.

The memory of my time in South Kensington takes me back to my days of schooling there. The prestigious building, which stood majestically ahead of me, symbolized the stepping stone to new beginnings. As I approached it, a sense of nostalgia washed over me, reminding me of the momentous decisions I made during my time within those walls.

Walking through the back streets of South Kensington, I retraced the path I used to take from the college building to the nearby train station.

Back then, I would envision the person I would become, the accomplishments I would achieve, and the impact I would make on the world. Now, standing in the same place, years later, I couldn't help but reflect on the person I once was and how far I had come.

The surrounding area, filled with exclusive clubs and high-end restaurants, exuded an air of sophistication and elegance. It is a place where the wealthy congregate, indulging in the finest things that life has to offer. The luxury that permeates every corner of this extravagant neighbourhood can almost be felt, as if it is woven into the very fabric of the buildings and streets.

Yet, as I walked through the streets, I couldn't help but think about the dichotomy of wealth that exists within this area. While some people bask in luxury and abundance, there are those who struggle to make ends meet just a few streets away. South Kensington serves as a vivid reminder of the stark contrasts that exist within our society, highlighting the immense inequalities that need to be addressed.

With the wind biting at my cheeks and the icy air seeping through every layer of my clothing, I embarked on what seemed like a daring adventure - walking from my current location to Knightsbridge, a neighbourhood famous for luxury shopping and designer brands. Opting for a leisurely stroll instead of the usual train ride, I immersed in a sea of bustling city life, each building adding fuel to my entrepreneurial dreams.

As I traversed the streets of London, the notable neighbourhoods and iconic landmarks morphed into a vivid portrait of what success could look like for Aluel Deng, my future London flagship store.

Observing the elegant architecture and luxurious storefronts, I couldn't help but imagine my own brand showcased prominently among the prosperous businesses of Knightsbridge. The extravagant dreams that I had harboured for my designer brand suddenly seemed within reach.

The walk allowed me to absorb the vibrant atmosphere and observe the determination of residents and shop owners in these coveted streets. They had created and cultivated their own thriving establishments, building successful enterprises from the ground up. Their perseverance and entrepreneurial spirit were evident in the polished facades and opulent window displays that lined the pavements.

With each passing minute, inspiration surged through my veins, dissolving any apprehensions that had previously lingered. If these individuals had achieved such grandeur, what was stopping me from joining their ranks? The fifteen-minute journey became a symbol of the potential that lay ahead - a tangible representation of the steps needed to transform my vision into a reality.

The biting cold no longer mattered as I envisioned Aluel Deng amidst the fashion giants and luxury retailers. I could visualize the elegance and sophistication that my brand would bring to this bustling hub of commerce. The determination within me grew stronger, fuelled by the realization that my dreams were not far-fetched or unattainable dreams, but rather, aspirations waiting to be fulfilled.

The walk also served as a reminder that success is not solely dependent on external factors, but on the grit and determination of the individual.

Everything around me showcased the boundless opportunities and possibilities that lay in wait, but it was ultimately up to me to seize them. The journey instilled in me a sense of confidence and self-assurance, reassuring me that if others could accomplish greatness, so could I.

Knightsbridge was no longer just a destination; it had become a symbol of the heights my plans could reach. The fifteen-minute walk had transformed from a seemingly arduous task into a catalyst of motivation. It had opened my eyes to the potential Aluel Deng possessed and ignited a fire within me to turn my dreams into a tangible reality.

In the end, my decision to walk instead of taking the train became a metaphor for my journey as an entrepreneur. It reminded me that success is not achieved by taking the path of least resistance, but by embracing the challenges and forging ahead with unwavering resilience.

# PRESSURE

Pressure is inevitable in the world of business.
Whether it is the pressure of meeting deadlines, managing
finances, dealing with competition, or satisfying clients,
entrepreneurs are faced with constant challenges.
However, the ability to handle pressure effectively can
determine the success or failure of an entrepreneur and
their company. To thrive in such a high-stress
environment, entrepreneurs need to adopt certain strategies
and approaches.

One of the most effective ways to handle pressure is by
allocating work to the right people. As a leader, it is
essential to have a team of skilled and reliable individuals
who can help share the workload. Delegating tasks to
competent team members not only lightens the burden on
the entrepreneur but also ensures that each task is handled
efficiently. This allows the entrepreneur to focus on more
critical aspects of the business and prevents them from
becoming overwhelmed by the pressure.

A key aspect of effectively handling pressure is taking a
step back and evaluating priorities. In the chaos of running
a business, it is easy to get caught up in the urgent but less
important tasks.

However, by taking a moment to assess what truly requires immediate attention, entrepreneurs can make better decisions about how to utilize their time and resources. This prioritization helps in preventing burnout and ensures that the most critical issues are addressed promptly.

Being able to maintain a healthy work-life balance is crucial when it comes to handling pressure effectively. Entrepreneurs often face long working hours, erratic schedules, and constant demands, but neglecting personal well-being can have detrimental effects on both mental and physical health. It is essential to set aside time for relaxation, exercise, hobbies, and spending time with loved ones. A well-rested and mentally rejuvenated entrepreneur is better equipped to handle pressure and make sound decisions.

In addition to these strategies, effective communication within the team and with external stakeholders is also essential in managing pressure. Clear communication about expectations, goals, and progress helps in minimizing misunderstandings and conflicts. Regular and open dialogue provides everyone involved with a sense of understanding and collaboration, making it easier to navigate through challenging situations.

As a whole, it is imperative for entrepreneurs to cultivate a positive mindset and develop resilience. Pressure is an inherent part of entrepreneurship, and setbacks and failures are bound to occur; but it is crucial not to let these obstacles consume and demotivate. Instead, entrepreneurs should view them as learning opportunities and stepping stones towards growth and success. Resilience allows entrepreneurs to bounce back from failures, adapt to changing circumstances, and maintain a positive attitude even in the face of immense pressure.

\*\*\*

Selena was a dedicated and hardworking assistant, there was no doubt about that. She had proven herself time and time again, taking on the overwhelming workload and ensuring that orders were processed efficiently and effectively. It was evident that she was committed to her job, but I couldn't help feeling sorry for her husband.

As a newlywed, one should be able to bask in the bliss of starting a life together, enjoying the initial days of marriage where everything seems perfect. But Selena was not able to experience this. Instead, she was constantly consumed by work, dedicating long hours to ensure that everything ran smoothly. Her dedication and sacrifice did not go unnoticed by me, and I couldn't help but think about the impact it had on her personal life.

On the other hand, I was a young woman with no hardcore personal responsibilities. My businesses were my babies, and I nurtured and cared for them with every ounce of my being. I understood the demands of running a business, and I knew that sometimes sacrifices had to be made. But I couldn't fully comprehend Selena's situation because I had never experienced it myself.

I didn't want to be unsympathetic or distant from Selena's struggles, but it was difficult to relate. I needed to find a solution that would alleviate the workload without compromising the quality of service we provided. That's when Selena suggested she come to London to assist me.

Although it was a kind offer, I declined. I didn't want Selena to uproot her life or sacrifice her time with her husband. I wanted her to have a balanced life, where work and personal life could coexist harmoniously.

So, I presented her with an alternative solution - hire another person to join our team or increase our working hours.

We both knew that the latter option was not ideal. We were already exerting ourselves to the maximum, and pushing ourselves even further would only lead to burnout. Therefore, the logical choice was to hire another team member who could share the workload and provide the necessary support.

In the end, Selena agreed. She understood that it was necessary for the growth and sustainability of our business. We began the process of searching for a suitable candidate who would fit seamlessly into our team dynamic. It was a challenging task, but we knew it was the right move.

The flood of orders was overwhelming, but with the addition of a new team member, we were able to better manage the workload. Selena's dedication and hard work were still invaluable, but she no longer had to bear the burden alone. We had created a support system that allowed us to maintain the quality of our services while still finding time for our personal lives.

Reflecting on this experience, I realized that empathy doesn't always come naturally. Sometimes, we need to put ourselves in someone else's shoes and make an effort to understand their struggles. In this case, I couldn't relate to Selena's situation, but I understood the importance of finding a solution that would benefit both the business and her personal life.

Running a successful business requires not only dedication and hard work but also compassion and understanding. I learned that sometimes, as a leader, I need to make difficult decisions that may not be ideal for everyone involved. But ultimately, it is these decisions that create an environment where everyone can thrive, both personally and professionally.

# RUMINATION

It can be a daunting experience when we are forced to confront our thoughts and the situations that have shaped our lives. Thoughts have a curious way of lingering in our minds, replaying events, revisiting conversations, and questioning our choices. Often, they leave us feeling worse for wear, as we find ourselves dwelling on past situations or scenarios that may have occurred at some point in our lives.

In these instances, we come face to face with the raw reality of our existence. We are confronted with the reasons why we do things the way we do, and sometimes, that truth can be cold and unforgiving. It can shake us to the core, making us question our past decisions, our present actions, and our future aspirations. Thoughts have a way of digging deep into our consciousness, exposing our vulnerabilities and frailties.

In the hustle and bustle of our daily lives, it is easy to push our life stories further and further away, compartmentalized in a tiny part of our brain. We immerse ourselves in work, relationships, and various distractions that offer temporary reprieve from self-reflection.

We bury ourselves under the weight of responsibilities, obligations, and societal expectations, hoping that by avoiding our thoughts, we can avoid facing our realities.

Despite our best efforts to suppress them, thoughts have a tendency to resurface, demanding our attention. They come knocking at the door of our consciousness, persistent and unyielding. Whether it is a regret from the past, a mistake that haunts us, or an unresolved issue, our thoughts have a way of intruding into our present moment, demanding that we acknowledge and address them.

When we finally muster the courage to face our thoughts, an array of emotions flood over us. We may experience sadness, regret, anger, or even despair. We feel the weight of our past choices, the consequences of our actions, and the possibilities that eluded us. Facing our thoughts requires us to confront our fears and accept our shortcomings. It demands that we peel back the layers of denial and pretence, exposing our authentic selves to scrutiny.

While acknowledging our thoughts can be painful, it also opens the door to growth and personal development. It allows us to understand ourselves better, to unravel the intricate web of factors that have shaped our lives. By facing our thoughts, we gain valuable insights into our patterns and behaviours, enabling us to make more informed choices in the future.

In the face of our thoughts, we begin to realize the value of self-reflection and introspection. We learn that it is not enough to simply exist; we must strive to understand ourselves, our motivations, and our desires.

By addressing our thoughts, we embark on a journey of self-discovery, peeling away the layers of self-doubt and insecurity, and embracing our strengths and capabilities.

\*\*\*

Still wandering the busy streets of Knightsbridge, it was a scenic moment exploring the high-end shops and indulging in the luxury that surrounded me. As I strolled along, taking in the sights and sounds, I couldn't help but feel a sense of detachment from the world around me. It was as if I was an observer, separate from the hustle and bustle of everyday life.

Checking my watch, I decided to take a moment to rest and reflect in a cosy little coffee shop before I made my way home. As I entered, the aroma of freshly brewed coffee filled the air, instantly soothing my senses. I ordered my usual latte and found a quiet corner table with a view of the rain-soaked streets outside.

As I sat there, sipping my latte and watching the droplets of rain cascade down the windowpane, my mind began to wander. I found myself contemplating the concept of hyper-independency, a trait that had come to define me over the years. Why was I so determined to rely solely on myself, consistently insistent to push away any help or support from others?

In the midst of my contemplation, my thoughts took an unexpected turn, leading me down the path of grief and loss. It was as if the rain outside was mirroring the tears that welled up in my eyes, for I had experienced a deep loss many years ago.

Tragically many years prior, I had lost both of my parents in a devastating plane crash, a sudden and unexpected blow that knocked the wind out of me. The grief was overwhelming, enveloping me in a darkness I never thought possible. In the aftermath, I found myself questioning the very core of my existence.

This unexpected loss had a profound effect on how I viewed the world. It was a wake-up call, a stark reminder that life can be cruel and unpredictable. It shattered my illusions of permanence, abruptly revealing the fragility of our existence. The realization hit me like a ton of bricks—I had to be prepared for the inevitable, for life waits for no one.

From that moment on, I became fiercely independent, determined to always be ready for whatever challenges life threw my way. I learned to rely on myself and only myself, unwilling to expose myself to the vulnerability that comes with relying on others. I built walls around my heart, shielding it from further pain and loss.

Sitting in that coffee shop, gazing out at the rain, I still began to question the validity of my hyper-independency. Was my fiercely self-reliant nature truly serving me, or was it preventing me from truly connecting with others? Was I denying myself the support and companionship that we as humans so desperately need?

As these thoughts swirled around in my mind, I realized that my grief had left an indelible mark on my perspective. While it had taught me valuable lessons about the fleeting nature of life, it had also caused me to isolate myself from the very world I yearned to be a part of.

It was in that coffee shop, surrounded by the gentle hum of conversation and the comforting scent of coffee, that I resolved to embrace vulnerability and open myself up to the possibilities of connection. I understood that while grief and loss can shape us, they must not define us. They provide the impetus for growth, but it is up to us to choose how we respond.

As I sipped the last remnants of my latte, I made a decision. I would allow myself to embrace vulnerability when needed, and to forge meaningful connections with those around me. Life may be uncertain, but it is also filled with joy. And it is in the shared experiences, the moments of connection, that we find solace and the courage to face whatever comes our way.

\*\*\*

Still sitting in the bustling coffee shop with a few more minutes to spare, memories of my deceased parents began to flood my mind, consuming me entirely. Thinking deeply about them, the two people who welcomed me into this world, who were no longer there to guide and support me, seemed to unlock a Pandora's box of emotions. It started innocently, with fond recollections of their love and care. But soon, darker memories began to creep in, ones that I had long suppressed and tried to forget.

With each sip, I dug deeper into every caved memory, slowly leaving the memories of my parents, now retrieving both significant and insignificant terrible events that had scarred my life. Painful experiences that I had pushed aside and promised myself never to revisit. Yet, there I was, willingly subjecting myself to the turmoil of those past grievances.

Realizing the dangerous path I was treading into, I shook myself out of that trap. I knew all too well where dwelling on the past could lead me. If I continued down this path of introspection, it could eventually plunge me into the depths of depression. The kind of depression that could paralyze my inner drive and wreak havoc on the businesses I had worked so hard to build. This was not a price I was ready or willing to pay.

In that moment, I mustered the courage to grasp the reality before me. Life had a knack for throwing an unfair share of pain, fury, and obstacles my way. But it did not define me. I still had a pulse, a life force that burned within me. I had to remind myself that my existence transcended the moments of anguish and heartache.

Every day was an opportunity to embrace the resilience that ran deep within me. Instead of being crushed by the weight of my past, I had the ability to rise above it. My parents, as much as I missed them, would have wanted me to live a life that honoured their memory. The love they bestowed upon me still lingered in the ether, guiding me forward.

Rather than getting lost in that abyss of despair, I chose to shift my focus towards the future. I reminded myself of the accomplishments I had achieved despite the challenges life had thrown my way. I equally reflected on the growth I had experienced as a result of those obstacles, emerging stronger and more determined each time. The gentle reminder in the coffee shop on the sombre day, left me to remember the journey won't be easy, but it will be worthwhile.

# VOYAGE

Travel is a remarkable experience that holds the power to transform individuals in ways unimaginable. Whether one embarks on a journey across the globe or simply exploring a neighbouring town, the act of traveling never fails to add value to our existence. It is through travel that we learn new things, gain fresh perspectives, and acquire an advantageous level of exposure that enables us to navigate the world with a newfound sense of wisdom.

One of the most enriching aspects of travel is the opportunity to learn. Every destination has its own unique history, culture, and people, and by immersing ourselves in these unfamiliar surroundings, we open ourselves up to a wealth of knowledge and understanding. We encounter new languages, customs, and traditions, all of which broaden our horizons and challenge our preconceived notions.

By delving into the depths of a different culture, we gain fresh perspectives that have the potential to revolutionize our own worldview. In our everyday lives, it can be easy to become trapped in the confines of our own routines and beliefs.

Adding to that, travel compels us to break free from these limitations and embrace alternative ways of living and thinking. We interact with individuals from diverse backgrounds, listen to their stories, and witness first-hand the beauty of cultural diversity. This exposure to different perspectives not only shapes our understanding of the world but also fosters empathy and tolerance within us. Travel leaves us constantly provided with an advantageous level of exposure that essentially makes us streetwise.

When we immerse ourselves in a foreign land, we are forced to navigate unfamiliar territories, understand local norms, and adapt to new situations. We develop a sense of resourcefulness, adaptability, and problem-solving skills that are invaluable in all aspects of life. The ability to connect with people from different walks of life and effectively communicate across linguistic and cultural barriers enables us to build strong relationships and opens doors for new opportunities.

Additionally, travel offers us peace and tranquillity that can be difficult to find in our fast-paced lives. Exploring new environments allows us to escape the monotony of our daily routines and reconnect with ourselves. Whether it is strolling through a vibrant market bustling with activity or finding solace in the serenity of nature, travel allows us to detach from our worries and embrace the present moment. These moments of peace not only rejuvenate our minds but also provide us with the space to reflect and grow as individuals.

While the benefits of travel are many, one of the most invaluable aspects is the constant education it provides. Every aspect of our surroundings becomes a source of instruction, from the historical landmarks that tell tales of -

the past to the local cuisine that teaches us about culinary traditions. Travel offers us the chance to constantly learn and grow, ensuring that our existence is never stagnant.

\*\*\*

In retrospect, 2022 was undeniably a turning point in my life, a year that I hold dear to my heart. It marked a paradigm shift, a realization that conforming to conventional societal measures and slaving away in a conventional job were not aligned with my true potential and aspirations. It was a year when I challenged the odds and charted my own path towards success and fulfilment.

Having acquired an extensive pool of knowledge in a remarkably short span of time, the idea of working as an employee no longer resonated with me. It felt like an insult to my intelligence to be confined within the boundaries of a hierarchical corporate structure. A defining experience during this period was witnessing the CEO of the company I was working for at some point, portraying cluelessness within numerous aspects of the business. It made me question my presence in that environment. If I felt that the person at the helm lacked essential understanding, then why was I willingly submitting myself to such an unfulfilling situation?

2022 also brought about an unexpected opportunity for me, one that not only added to my monthly income, but also empowered me to exercise my unparalleled confidence and ambition. It was the year I decided to purchase a forty feet shipping container and lease it out to a third-party company.

This venture materialized not only from a desire for financial stability but also as a means to position myself precisely where I wanted to be at that very moment. The decision to invest in a shipping container was not made lightly. It came as a result of careful consideration and thorough research into the feasibility and profitability of such an undertaking. This investment proved to be a strategic move, allowing me to diversify my sources of income and gain a level of financial stability that I had always yearned for.

Beyond the monetary gains, this venture also served as a testament to my unwavering confidence in my abilities. It was a tangible proof that I could break free from the chains of mediocrity and carve a path that aligned with my true potential. The decision to take the leap into entrepreneurship and create my own opportunities was not without its challenges, but it was a choice I made with conviction and determination.

As the end of the year unfolded, I discovered that my newfound ambition was a compass to what I needed to achieve. It propelled me forward, granting me the resilience and tenacity to overcome obstacles. I embraced every challenge as an opportunity for growth and transformation.

***

As I stood at the bustling London Heathrow airport, ready to embark on yet another journey to South Sudan, nostalgia hit me like a brick wall. Waving goodbye to the mundane of the UK, I was ready to fully immerse myself once again in the vibrant and dynamic culture that awaited me. It was the dawn of a new year, and the possibilities ahead seemed endless.

Unlike my previous trip to South Sudan in 2020, this time I was accompanied by a close friend. We had both come a long way in our respective careers, excelling and achieving our goals. This added a whole new dimension to our trip, as we were both embarking on a new chapter in our lives.

South Sudan, a land of resilience and sheer beauty, was more than just a destination for me; it held a special place in my heart. Over the years, I had developed a deep connection with the country and its people. From the moment I first stepped on its soil, I was captivated.

As our journey began, we boarded the plane, ready to be transported to Juba. The anticipation of what awaited us upon our arrival filled the air. The familiar hum of the aircraft engines resonated with my excitement, as I thought about the experiences and adventures that lay ahead.

The plane ride was fun, perhaps it was the simple fact that I wasn't alone, and accompanied by my friend. We laughed at trivial matters and spoke deeply about various important topics. As someone who struggles to sleep when on a flight, I flicked through movies on the in-flight entertainment system as my friend slept. I had butterflies in my stomach once again. It always happens this way as I make my way to my home country. Nervousness? I don't know.

My journey to South Sudan was not just a physical one; it was an emotional and mental pilgrimage. It was a return to my roots, a reconnection with my heritage, and an acknowledgment of the struggles faced by my people. I was filled with a sense of responsibility and purpose to contribute, even in a small way, to the betterment of the country.

Despite the turbulence in my mind, there was also a sense of hope that accompanied me on this journey. It is the hope that things have changed, that progress has been made, and that my efforts, however modest, can make a difference. South Sudan is a place of immense challenges, but it is also a place of resilience, courage, and determination.

The warmth radiating from everyone's faces was palpable from the moment we landed in Juba. We were greeted by friendly faces, eager to welcome us back with open arms. The city had transformed since my last visit, with new developments and infrastructure springing up at every corner. It was a testament to the resilience and determination of the South Sudanese; despite the challenges they had faced over the years.

The days were filled with enriching experiences and encounters with the people of South Sudan. We explored the vibrant markets, sampling local delicacies and immersing ourselves in the rich cultural heritage. We witnessed traditional dances and listened to stories passed down through generations, adding layers of appreciation for our culture.

Charity, often associated with kindness, compassion, and giving, is a virtue that resonates with the human heart. It is a noble act that not only helps those in need but also brings satisfaction and fulfilment to the giver. There is an old saying that charity starts at home, and my recent experience in the vibrant city of Juba reaffirmed the significance of this adage.

As I strolled through the bustling streets of Juba, I found myself captivated by the harmonious voices of a group of young boys singing and playing near a car wash.

Their talent and enthusiasm were truly awe-inspiring, and it was evident that they had been honing their skills for quite some time. Their impromptu performance attracted a small crowd of onlookers, all of whom were equally enthralled by their exceptional talent.

While their performance had deeply moved me, it was their persistent efforts to sell me various products that left a lasting impression on my mind. With the Arabic I knew to get by, I managed to politely decline their offer, with instead, a counteroffer. I was determined to make a small difference in the lives of these young boys, who had displayed such immense talent and enthusiasm; mostly to teach them an invaluable lesson that life is harsh, but people can be kind.

In that moment, I decided to depart from the traditional notion of charity and instead opt for a more personal and direct form of assistance. I wanted to ensure that my contribution would have a direct impact on their lives, even if it were just for a brief period of time.
With this in mind, I made sure to offer them cash assistance that would cover their food expenses for at least two to three weeks.

Seeing their eyes light up with gratitude was a priceless experience. I realized that sometimes, it takes just a small gesture of kindness to bring happiness to someone's life. As I bid them farewell, I gave each of them a high five, hoping to leave a lasting memory of our encounter.

Continuing my journey to meet friends at a nearby restaurant, my heart was filled with a sense of contentment and satisfaction. The saying "charity starts at home" had taken on a new depth of meaning for me.

It reminded me that acts of charity should not be limited to grand gestures or public demonstrations but should also extend to our immediate surroundings, our communities, and the people we encounter in our day-to-day lives.

Charity, after all, is about cultivating empathy and extending a helping hand to those who need it the most. It does not always require tremendous resources or a global platform; it simply requires a compassionate heart and a willingness to make a difference, no matter how small.

Moments after my friends and I decided to indulge in the pleasure of dining outdoors, I found myself unexpectedly greeted by fellow diners who recognized me and appreciated my work. This experience was especially humbling since it took place in my home country, where I had built a reputation for my excelling work ethic. As I sat with my friends, catching up on life and sharing laughter, contentment consumed me.

However, even in the midst of this joyous occasion, the responsibilities of my professional life never left my thoughts. Knowing that I needed to stay connected to my business, I made a spontaneous decision to reach out to my accountant, informing him of my presence in town and suggesting a meeting. Understanding the importance of keeping up with the progress and prospects of the business, I felt it necessary to consult with him, especially considering my physical absence in the country for some time.

To my satisfaction, he promptly responded affirmatively to my proposition, eager to discuss any updates and developments pertaining to the business.

With this confirmation, I bid my friends farewell, promising to return soon, and headed towards a local coffee shop to meet with him.

Entering the coffee shop, the coffee filled air overwhelmed the room, comforting my senses and setting the stage for our business conversation. As I spotted my accountant sitting at a corner table, engrossed in his paperwork, I couldn't help but appreciate his dedication and professionalism.

Taking a seat opposite him, I was greeted with a warm smile and a sense of familiarity that alluded to the long working relationship we had cultivated over the years. Without wasting any time, we delved right into the discussion, eager to exchange information and insights that would shape the course of our business.

Our conversation was a mix of reviewing financial statements, analysing market trends, and assessing the competition. As my accountant provided a detailed account of the fiscal progress during my absence, I listened intently, occasionally interjecting with inquiries and suggestions. It was reassuring to have someone who comprehended the intricacies of my business and could offer sound advice.

The coffee shop, with its lively ambiance and soft background music, served as the ideal setting for our meeting. The casual yet professional atmosphere allowed us to converse freely, exchanging ideas and strategies to propel the business forward.

As the afternoon progressed, our discussions became more animated and filled with renewed enthusiasm.

We brainstormed innovative approaches and contemplated potential collaborations that could further enhance the growth of the business. The coffee, still warm and comforting, seemed to fuel our creativity and ignite a fresh sense of determination.

Leaving the coffee shop, I felt invigorated and reassured about the future of my business. The meeting with my accountant had not only provided me with vital information on the current state of affairs but had also reaffirmed the importance of staying connected and engaged in the progress of my company.

Reflecting on that day, despite initially planning for a leisurely get-together with friends, I had seized the opportunity to nurture my business and stay informed. This experience reinforced the notion that business responsibilities are ever-present, and a successful enterprise demands both dedication and timely decision-making.

As I subsequently re-joined my friends to resume our gathering, I couldn't help but express gratitude for the unexpected turn of events. This impromptu meeting had reminded me of the significance of balancing work and personal life and the rewards that come with it. It had also reinforced the value of recognizing and acknowledging the impact one's work can have on others, reiterating the importance of humility and gratitude.

During our time together, I noticed the joy that radiated from each person's face. Laughter filled the air, smiles were contagious, and the warmth of companionship was tangible.

It quickly became apparent that the rewards of spending quality time with loved ones far outweighed any accomplishment attained through work alone. The moment we shared during this impromptu meeting was a true testament to the sentiment of community.

As I observed the individuals in our gathering, I couldn't help but notice how their faces formed expressive communication with mostly happiness as we engaged in conversations, shared stories, and reminisced about old times. Laughter erupted frequently, lifting the spirits of everyone present. It was as if a weight had been lifted off our shoulders, and that was a needed indirect therapy session.

The smiles on their faces were contagious, spreading from one person to another like wildfire. It was a beautiful sight to behold, witnessing the transformative power of genuine human connection.

# FAMILY

The importance of family cannot be overstated. It serves as a source of protection for various elements of our lives, including our mental, emotional, spiritual, financial, and physical well-being. Maintaining a healthy relationship with a trusted family member can be the saving grace in moments when we least expect it.

In the conventional home setup, it is within the walls of our homes that we find support and understanding. In times of stress or uncertainty, being able to turn to a family member who genuinely cares about our mental health can provide a sense of comfort and stability. A family member's presence and ability to offer a listening ear can alleviate anxiety and promote mental well-being.

Emotionally, family acts as a safety net. They are the ones who know us intimately, often understanding our emotions even before we do. During times of sadness, grief, or overwhelming joy, family members can provide the emotional support we need. They offer a shoulder to cry on, celebrate our successes, and provide a sense of unconditional love that is difficult to find elsewhere. This emotional protection strengthens our resilience to help us navigate life's challenges.

Spiritually, family can serve as a guiding force. Having a shared belief system or religious practices within the family can provide a sense of purpose and meaning in life. Families that engage in spiritual activities together, such as attending religious services or practicing meditation, create a supportive environment for the growth and development of one's spiritual well-being. The shared values and beliefs inherent in family life offer protection and guidance in navigating the complexities of the world.

Financial security is another aspect in which family can provide protection. Families often pool resources to offer assistance during times of financial hardship. Whether it be loans, shelter, or financial advice, family members are willing to help shoulder the burden. This support system can alleviate the stress associated with financial struggles and provide a sense of stability. It is reassuring to know that you have a safety net in place, which will catch you if you happen to fall.

Lastly, family can safeguard us physically. In times of danger, illness, or unexpected trouble, having family members who prioritize our safety is invaluable. They go to great lengths to ensure our physical well-being, acting as a shield against harm. Whether it be providing shelter, taking care of us when we are unwell, or ensuring we are in a safe environment, family takes significant steps to protect us from physical harm.

We never know when life may throw us a curveball, so having someone we can rely on is essential to weathering the storm. One we simply cannot do alone.

***

My older siblings and I have always shared a bond that goes beyond the typical sibling relationship. We were not only connected by blood, but also by a deep sense of care, and understanding. This connection became even stronger after the loss of our parents, as we leaned on each other for support and strength during those difficult times.

Growing up, our family was tightly knit. We were allies... confidants to one another. Our parents had instilled in us the values of love, compassion, and unity, which served as the foundation for the strong bond we developed. From childhood, we were always there for each other, whether it was helping with homework, offering guidance, or simply lending an empathetic ear.

One of the things that brought us even closer together was the way we planned and celebrated family holidays. We would gather around the dining table to discuss and decide the perfect destination for our vacations. The excitement and anticipation of the upcoming holidays would fill the air, and we would spend hours researching and exploring different options to make our family trips memorable. These planning sessions were not just about choosing a destination; they were valuable moments of togetherness.

Christmas was always an extra special time for us. We would bellow with laughter as we prepared dinner, whilst our nieces would help themselves to the sweet treats laying on the dining table. On Christmas morning, the joy and excitement of unwrapping presents filled the room, but the true essence of our celebration was the love and appreciation we had for each other.

Our family gatherings were never dull or small; they were vibrant and filled with laughter, stories, and a genuine sense of belonging.

We were truly blessed to have each other during those holiday seasons.

Beyond the festivities, our connection as siblings ran deep. Whenever one of us faced a challenge or needed support, we would rally together to lend a helping hand. The loss of our parents only amplified this bond. We became each other's pillars of strength, supporting one another through grief and uncertainty. During tough times, we leaned on our shared experiences and memories, reminding ourselves that we were not alone in this journey.

The role that my older siblings played in my life cannot be overstated. They became my protectors, my teachers, and my role models. They guided me through the highs and lows of life, ensuring that I felt loved, valued, and supported. Their presence was a constant reminder that I was never alone; I had a family that would always be there for me.

I consider myself incredibly fortunate to have been born into the family that I was. The values we were taught when younger brought us even closer, reinforcing the importance of cherishing the bond we were taught to never break. My siblings had taught me the true meaning of resilience after loss. We continued to navigate life's challenges together, knowing that our bond continued to provide us with the strength to overcome any obstacle.

They say that the apple doesn't fall too far from the tree. Sometimes, I wonder if another reason why I fell so deeply in love with the line of business was because I was born into a family that had an insatiable hunger for ambition. There was an undeniable drive and determination that I witnessed from my parents, siblings, and the entire household. It was this drive that propelled me towards discovering my own passion and success in the business world.

My mother, a strong and resilient woman, immigrated from South Sudan to the United Kingdom in the early 90's with a handful of children in tow, leaving my father behind to fight for the freedom of our country.

She understood the importance of financial stability and worked tirelessly to provide for our family. From an early age, I watched her line up a stream of businesses to sustain the household income. From small start-ups to established ventures, she never shied away from exploring new opportunities. Witnessing her unwavering dedication and entrepreneurial spirit instilled in me a deep admiration for her work ethic.

My father, too, had his fair share of struggles and triumphs. Like my mother, he eventually immigrated to the UK in the mid 90's, wanting to reunite with his family. He opened a convenience store in the heart of London, facing every obstacle head-on and working long hours to establish a stable income source. His sacrifice for the people of South Sudan was not too long recognized, and he was later rewarded by being appointed as the first Minister of Defence for South Sudan. His journey taught me that diligence will always be rewarded.

As I grew older, I witnessed the entrepreneurial ventures of my siblings, further reinforcing the idea that success in the world of business was not only attainable but also expected in our household. Each of them started and succeeded in multiple businesses, proving that ambition ran through our blood. From successful enterprises to tech-based start-ups, they paved the way for my own aspirations.

It seemed that I was destined to follow in their footsteps and equally achieve greatness.

The drive and resilience I saw around me served as a constant reminder that success was possible, as long as I put in the hard work and pursued my ambitions wholeheartedly. The family environment I grew up in was one of constant support and belief in our individual and collective abilities. I felt a sense of duty and responsibility to contribute to our legacy of ambition and success.

Being raised in a well-run household has undoubtedly shaped my perspective on how I envision running my own family in the future. The privilege of belonging to such a remarkable family has left me wondering whether the family I create will be equally blessed. As I embark on this journey, I am compelled to reflect on the values instilled in me, the lessons learned, and the aspirations I have for my own household.

From a young age, I witnessed everyone around me wholeheartedly pursue their dreams. Their unwavering dedication to their careers has not only provided us with a comfortable life but also imparted a sense of purpose and determination. This example has taught me the importance of setting goals, working diligently towards achieving them, and never settling for mediocrity.

I also realized the significance of structure and organization. My parents had managed to create an environment that fosters discipline, balance, and productivity. Each family member had specific responsibilities to fulfil, especially within their personal lives, and expectations were set high. This framework not only ensured that the household functioned smoothly but also instilled a sense of accountability.

Would I be able to create an equally blessed family someday?

A household is not only characterized by financial stability but also by an abundance of love, support, and opportunity. I was provided with access to quality education, extracurricular activities, and a nurturing environment that allowed me to flourish. As I consider my future family, I question whether I will be able to replicate this level of fortune and create an environment that fosters growth and happiness.

However, contemplating these questions also made me realize that it is not solely about material blessings or financial wealth. The true measure of success lies in the values, principles, and love that bind a family together. It is about creating a space where every member feels supported, and most equally, safe. It is about fostering an environment where growth, learning, and personal development are prioritized. In this light, the blessings bestowed upon my family are not solely due to external factors, but rather a result of the love, unity, and shared values that define us.

As I envision my own household, I aspire to prioritize the same values that have been integral to my upbringing. I want to create a home where ambition is nurtured, goals are encouraged, and dedication is instilled in every aspect of life. I believe in creating a structure that promotes productivity, balance, and responsibility, allowing each member to thrive and contribute to the overall well-being of the family. I aspire to provide my future family with opportunities, support, and love, enabling them to explore their passions and reach their full potential.

Ultimately, while it is natural to compare my future family to the one I was blessed to be born into, I understand that every family has its unique dynamics and challenges.

The lessons learned from my upbringing have given me the tools to build a strong foundation for the family I hope to create. By nurturing ambition, instilling values, and fostering the love of God, I am confident that my future household will be filled with blessings of its own, even if they may be different from those I experienced growing up.

*\*\**

As the evening approached and the sun lazily descended behind the horizon in Juba, I bid farewell to my friends and set out to meet my brother-in-law at a popular hangout spot. The contrasting experiences of a dark, yet warm evening in Juba, in comparison to the chilly evenings I had left behind in England left me astounded.

As we reunited, my brother-in-law couldn't help but tease me about my previous extended stays in South Sudan. He jokingly remarked, "Are you sure you're going back to London in two weeks? Last time you said that, you stayed another hundred!". We both erupted into laughter, realizing the truth behind his words. It was undeniable that my time in South Sudan had a profound impact on me, evident from the radiant glow on my face.

After a long day, as exhaustion slowly weighed me down, I decided to retire back home and seek solace in the comfort of my bed. As I laid there, I instinctively reached for my phone, unable to resist the need to check it one last time before I closed my eyes. Little did I know that a simple action would fill my heart with warmth and love.

A gentle ping drew my attention to a new message. Curiosity sparked within me as I unlocked my phone, wondering who would reach out to me at this hour.

To my delight, it was a message from my sister, who was in London, many miles away. In that moment, the distance that separated us became inconsequential.

Opening the message, I discovered a delightful surprise - it was a video of my adorable niece, spontaneously singing along to a Disney movie. With each note, her voice radiated pure innocence and joy. My heart swelled with pride as I watched her perform with such passion.

In that fleeting moment, as the video played before me, I realized the significance of what it truly meant. There was an indirect solace and happiness in sharing moments of happiness with one another. And that's what it was all about. The essence of family.

# CONCEPT

We often find ourselves stuck in a rut, unable to move forward or take action on our ideas. In those moments, it is easy to blame the lack of inspiration for our inaction. We wait for that magical spark of creativity to ignite within us, longing for it to reveal the path we were meant to take. However, what if I were to tell you that the answer is often right in front of us, waiting to be recognized and embraced?

Gone are the days when trial and error was the sole foundation of success in business. We live in an age where information is readily available, resources are abundant, and success stories serve as blueprints for our own endeavours. With endless sources of inspiration surrounding us, it is essential to look beyond the traditional confines and explore the possibilities that lie before us.

The world we live in is teeming with potential and opportunities. It is crucial to acknowledge that inspiration can take many forms. It can be found in conversations with friends, observations in nature, or even in the curious mind of a child.

Inspiration may also strike while reading a book, watching a movie, or listening to a captivating piece of music. These seemingly ordinary moments can hold the key to unlocking our potential and leading us down the path we were meant to take.

It is important to acknowledge that inspiration alone is not enough. The initiative to act on our ideas is equally crucial. It's so easy to find ourselves waiting for the perfect opportunity or the right moment to do something we've been meaning to do; but we must remember that success favours those who take action and seize the moment. We must be willing to take risks, step out of our comfort zones, and embrace the unknown.

When we restrict ourselves to conventional thinking or stay within our self-imposed limitations, we miss out on bigger and better opportunities. By opening our eyes and expanding our horizons, we can uncover hidden possibilities and untapped potential. The answer we seek is often waiting just beyond the edge of our comfort zone, and it is up to us to take the leap and explore the unknown.

Believe it or not, it is essential to recognize that inspiration is a continuous process. It is not a one-time event but a lifelong journey. We must remain open-minded and constantly seek new sources of inspiration to fuel our ideas and goals. The answer may not always come immediately or in the form we expect, but by remaining receptive, we allow ourselves to evolve.

*\*\**

Being an avid perfume enthusiast, I have always been captivated by the power of scent and its ability to influence our mood, evoke memories, and make a striking impression.

From an early age, I found myself captivated by the enchanting world of perfumes and their intricate blend of scents. The way perfumes have the power to transport us to different times and places, invoke memories, and evoke emotions fascinated me.

The allure of fragrance has always been strong; its significance spans across cultures and history. Perfumes have been coveted and cherished by civilizations throughout the centuries. They have adorned pharaohs in ancient Egypt, adorned the bodies of emperors in Rome, and been treasured as symbols of opulence and elegance in the royal courts of Europe.

As I delved deeper into the world of perfumery, I wanted to create a new scent, richer than previously created, that would not only enchant the senses but also pay homage to the rich cultural heritage of the regions that inspired it. It was during my travels and encounters with women in countries such as South Sudan and the United Arab Emirates that I began to understand the common scent they adorned themselves with - the majestic aroma of Oudh.

Oudh, also known as agarwood, is a resinous and highly aromatic wood found in Southeast Asia. Its scent is opulent, captivating, and often associated with luxury. Inspired by the regal allure of Oudh, I embarked on a journey of deep research and exploration, determined to craft a perfume that would truly capture its essence.

The Regal fragrance, the first product that graced Aluel Deng, the brand, was nothing short of majestic. Opening with top notes of citrus and floral accords, it gracefully transitions into a heart of rich spices and woods, creating an alluring and sophisticated blend.

The base notes of Oudh and musk left a lingering trail of opulence, reminiscent of timeless elegance.

As the creator of this fragrance, I not only wanted it to be a representation of my brand but also a scent that my customer's would genuinely enjoy wearing. To ensure its authenticity, I wore Regal religiously, allowing it to become a part of my daily routine. The perfume became a testament to the quality and craftsmanship of my brand, an embodiment of the passion and dedication I poured into its creation.

Whether you found yourself walking the bustling streets of a vibrant city or attending a glamorous event, the perfume had the power to transport you to a world of opulence and extravagance. It was a scent that knew no limits, effortlessly captivating the attention of all those who come in contact with it.

Creating a successful brand requires constant innovation and the ability to identify and fulfil unmet customer needs. As an entrepreneur, it is essential to have the intuition to recognize opportunities for expansion and growth. Leading me to a discovery during my recent visit to Juba, when I discovered an untapped potential in the fragrance market, knowing I wanted to explore it further.

While in Juba, I had many epiphanies - the need to expand on Regal being a significant one. The fragrance was captivating, but I couldn't help but feel that there was room for improvement. The idea of a richer and more luxurious tweaked version of this perfume, as an oil instead of an eau de parfum, seeded itself in my mind, and I eagerly awaited my return to the UK, where I planned to bring this concept to life.

Recognizing the importance of customer research in the development of new products, I utilized my time in Juba to conduct a mental survey. I observed the scents worn by the people I interacted with, paying particular attention to women. By mentally noting the fragrances that filled the air as I hugged friends and passed by strangers, I began to categorize them into distinct fragrance profiles: sweet, floral, and masculine.

At the end of each day, I took some time to reflect on my observations and analyse the common scent preferences of the city's inhabitants. This process enabled me to gain a deeper understanding of the fragrance notes that resonated with the people of Juba. Armed with this knowledge, I knew exactly which aromatic elements I needed to incorporate into the brand's perfume oil to create a product that would appeal to the local market.

With the goal of launching the oil-based version of the perfume as the second product within my brand, I set out to make this vision a reality. Drawing towards my entrepreneurial know-how, I understood the importance of carefully selecting and blending fragrance notes to create an enticing and unique scent. I collaborated with perfumers globally who shared my passion for quality and innovation, working relentlessly to craft a perfect mix that embodied the sophistication that I envisioned.

By understanding the preferences of the consumers in Juba, I was confident in my ability to design a perfume oil that would not only resonate with the local market but also exceed their expectations. I knew that this eventual expansion would be a strategic move for my brand, allowing me to enter a new market segment and cater to a wider range of customers.

When I returned to London, a surge of fascination came upon me on how the cultures I had experienced in my journey had left such a profound impact on my thoughts and ideas. As I sat back at my drawing board with Selena on the other end of the phone, I realized that my fresh perspective on the world had sparked a fire within me to expand.

As we delved into brainstorming sessions, ideas began to flow like a river. It was no longer a struggle to come up with innovative concepts; instead, it felt like we had tapped into an infinite reservoir of creativity. The exposure to different lifestyles, customs, and traditions had expanded our minds, allowing us to see beyond the boundaries of our local environment.

One of the major aspects we revised was the product ideas. We began incorporating elements inspired by the diverse cultures I had encountered. From the intricate designs of traditional crafts to the nostalgic aromas that filled various environments, my business started to take shape as a melting pot of global inspirations. We sought to bring forth the essence of various cultures while ensuring the products remained accessible and relatable to a wider audience.

With my newfound inspiration, I meticulously crafted execution plans; understanding that it was not just about having great ideas, but also about effectively implementing them. Specific and measurable goals were set, breaking down the process into smaller, achievable tasks. The time frame allocated allowed me to envision the progress and prioritize all efforts accordingly.

Understanding the various marketing techniques played a crucial role in shaping my business model.

The exposure to different advertising strategies during my travels helped us to think beyond the conventional methods. We explored the power of storytelling, incorporating narratives that resonated with the cultural influences behind the products. Social media platforms served as a canvas, allowing a connection with like-minded individuals who appreciated the richness of diverse cultures.

As we worked tirelessly on the new model of business, it became apparent that previous global experiences were the driving force behind the brand. Each country visited had unravelled unique aspects of human existence and taught us valuable lessons.

I also realized that the awareness came with a responsibility. In this interconnected era, it was crucial to acknowledge and respect the cultures that had inspired me. As the face and brain of the brand, I made it a point to collaborate with local artisans, ensuring that their skills were appreciated and preserved. By doing this, was the creation of a business that not only celebrated cultural diversity but also supported the communities that had contributed to my ideas.

# IMPRACTICALITY

Dreams are a powerful force that drive individuals to reach for the stars and achieve greatness. They ignite passion and motivate us to push our boundaries in pursuit of our deepest desires. In the realm of imagination, we have the freedom to create any plotline or scenario we desire. We can envision ourselves as superheroes, inventors, or even magicians - but the key lies in understanding the limitations of our abilities and circumstances. Just as a bus driver cannot suddenly fly a plane, or a mathematician cannot perform surgeries without proper training, there are certain boundaries that restrict our capabilities.

While it is true that with time and effort, these boundaries can be broken and seemingly impossible feats can become a reality, it is important to acknowledge that this process takes time. Rushing into unrealistic goals without acquiring the necessary skills, knowledge, or resources can lead to disastrous consequences. It is crucial to evaluate the feasibility of our dreams and set realistic expectations for ourselves.

The same holds true in the realm of business. Generating profit is undoubtedly a significant achievement, but it does not automatically guarantee instant riches.

It is tempting to make impulsive financial decisions based solely on the desire for quick monetary gain; however, this mindset often leads to grave mistakes and financial ruin. It is essential to assess the risks and rewards of each decision, considering the long-term implications rather than short-term gains.

Successful entrepreneurs understand the importance of making informed decisions based on careful analysis and a deep understanding of the market. They do not succumb to the allure of instant gratification but instead focus on building sustainable and profitable ventures over time. They are aware that impractical ambitions can lead to significant destruction, both personally and professionally.

In the pursuit of our dreams, it is crucial to maintain a sense of realism. This does not mean compromising on our ambitions or settling for mediocrity. On the contrary, it means being aware of our limitations and recognizing the steps required to bridge the gap between our current reality and our desired future. It involves setting practical goals, breaking them down into manageable steps, and continuously reassessing our progress to ensure we stay on track.

***

The revived business plan was a ray of hope in my levelled journey as an entrepreneur. It represented a culmination of years of hard work, perseverance, and the unwavering belief in my brand. I had a clear vision of how I wanted my brand to be perceived and how I intended to bring my ideas to life. Gone were the days of being a novice and merely enthralled by the idea of starting a business. I had transformed into an engine of innovation, the ambassador of tenacity.

The excitement that accompanied the revived business plan was electric. It coursed through every fibre of my being, driving me to delve deeper into my imagination and envision what my brand could become. With each passing moment, my enthusiasm grew, fuelling my determination to turn my dreams into reality.

Engrossed in deep thought, an idea had captivated my imagination—a store in the upscale neighbourhood of Knightsbridge. It was a place I had visited a month prior and fell in love with. The ambiance was perfect, and it had all the elements I envisioned for my brand. As I began searching for rental prices for these stores, I was greeted with astonishment. The figures were exorbitant, far beyond what I had expected. But a small voice inside me refused to be deterred, telling me, "You can do it. You can have that store in two months. Just believe."

Despite this voice urging me to take the leap, I knew I had to be realistic and practical in my assessment. I began piecing together the financial information I had on all my businesses. It soon became apparent that acquiring that store, especially within that locality, would be a severe financial strain. The numbers told a different story—a tale of substantial losses rather than the fruitful endeavour I had envisioned. What initially seemed like a dream, now assumed the form of a proliferating headache.

It was a challenging realization to accept, as it meant relinquishing my dream, at least for now. Reflecting on the larger picture, I had to prioritize sustainability and financial viability over the allure of a prestigious location. Expansion should not come at the cost of the overall health of the business.

Disappointment coursed through my veins, momentarily dampening my spirits, but as always, I swiftly reminded myself that setbacks and adaptations are inherent in the journey of entrepreneurship. This realization spurred me to engage in critical thinking and devise alternative strategies to achieve my brand's growth while maintaining financial stability.

With renewed determination, I set out to explore other opportunities and avenues that would align with my business goals and financial capabilities. This situation in particular became an impetus for creativity as I began searching for ways to expand my brand's reach without compromising its potential for success.

\*\*\*

As the demands of unrealistic, intensive thoughts continued to accumulate, I realized that I needed a quick break. Also, a break from the never-ending emails, the constant deadlines, and the overwhelming stress that had been weighing me down. So, on a particularly sunny afternoon, I made the conscious decision to indulge in some much-needed self-care and relaxation.

As I stood in the kitchen, I found myself drawn towards the comforting aroma of Earl Grey tea wafting through the air as I stirred the mug. There was something about the fragrant citrus notes and the warmth of the teacup that enticed me. Having always been a fan of tea, it was no surprise that Earl Grey was my absolute favourite. Its soothing qualities had become my go-to remedy during moments of chaos.

Feeling adventurous, I decided to pair my cup of tea with a South Sudanese snack I loved, called legamat.

These sugary bite-sized, deep-fried balls of cooked dough are often enjoyed alongside a cup of tea. Their golden-brown exterior and soft, fluffy interior created a perfect harmony with the aromatic tea.

Each bite was a symphony of flavours, as the indulgent sweetness of the legamat melded exquisitely with the subtle bergamot undertones of the Earl Grey.

Eager to savour this delightful combination, I carefully carried my precious treats up the stairs, making my way back to the sanctuary of my bedroom. With my warm cup of tea in one hand and a plate of legamat in the other, I settled onto my indulgently comfortable bed, ready to immerse myself in a world far removed from my own.

Flipping through the channels on my television, I stumbled upon an aviation documentary. To my surprise, I realized that I had always been inexplicably drawn to anything related to airplanes and the wonders of flight. Maybe in a past life, I thought to myself, I was a pilot, soaring through the skies with grace and precision. Perhaps I was an aircraft mechanic, tirelessly ensuring the safety of those who entrusted their lives to the metal birds. Or maybe, just maybe, I was an aerospace engineer, pushing the boundaries of innovation and exploration.

As the documentary unfolded before my eyes, I found myself captivated by every detail. The sleek design of the aircraft, the intricate mechanics propelling them forward, and the astounding physics that allowed them to defy gravity. I was in awe of the human ingenuity and determination that have propelled us into the age of flight. Here, in the confines of my bedroom, I was transported to a world where limits did not exist, and dreams took flight.

In that moment, my mind was fully engaged, and yet, at total peace. The worries and stresses of the outside world faded into the background, replaced by a profound sense of tranquillity. It was just me, my tea, the legamat, and this captivating glimpse into the realm of aviation.

As the documentary came to an end, I sat there in silence, reflecting on the serendipity of this afternoon's escape. The simple act of taking a break from work had led me to total serenity. It had reminded me of the importance of indulging in the things we love, of allowing ourselves to be completely present in the moment, and of finding solace in our passions.

So, as I placed my then empty teacup aside, I felt, simply, complete.

Sometimes, all it takes is a warm cup of tea, a flavourful snack, and an unexpected source of entertainment to remind us of the beauty of life, even in its simplest moments.

# RISK

When it comes to tradesmanship, there is a delicate balance between realism and impracticality. While it is essential to have a grounded understanding of the market and its dynamics, it is equally important to take risks in order to stand out and make a mark. Without risk, an individual cannot truly embody the spirit of an entrepreneur, which comes with knowing the crucialness to set the financial space for failure, accommodating this risk - as even if it doesn't work out, it would not have a profound impact on their life. The only thing that may cause frustration is the loss of time, as time is an element that cannot be recovered.

Realism is a trait that every entrepreneur must possess. It involves understanding the existing market conditions, the demand for products or services, and the potential competition. Realism helps in setting achievable goals and formulating strategies that are based on a practical understanding of the industry. It allows individuals to make informed decisions and avoid irrational or impractical endeavours.

Taking risks without having a financial cushion can be a daunting proposition.

Failure without adequate financial backing can leave severe consequences, leading to financial ruin or bankruptcy. That is why having the financial space for failure is paramount. It means having the resources and support systems in place to withstand potential losses. It is about minimizing the impact of failure and ensuring that setbacks do not have a long-lasting negative effect. By doing this, entrepreneurs can take calculated risks.

These risks can lead to the emergence of unique ideas, ground-breaking products, and innovative solutions. Having a safety net not only mitigates the fear of failure but also encourages boldness and experimentation. It allows entrepreneurs to push their boundaries, try new things, and learn from both successes and failures. Failure becomes a stepping stone to growth and serves as a valuable learning experience.

It is equally essential to recognize that the most valuable resource that an entrepreneur has is time. Time is finite, and once it's gone, it is irretrievable. Losing time without achieving significant progress can be frustrating and disheartening, presenting its importance that entrepreneurs must strike a balance between taking calculated risks and being mindful of the time and resources invested.

***

The wholesaler factory was bustling with activity as I stepped inside. The walls were adorned with bolts of vibrant and richly coloured fabrics, each one telling its own story. As I navigated through the maze-like rows, it became apparent that finding the perfect silk fabric for my brand's clothing collection was not going to be an easy task.

I approached a salesman, eager to begin my search. Having done my research beforehand, I knew that pure silk would be the ideal fabric to bring my vision to life. I requested to see samples in white and cream, knowing that these neutral tones would allow me to envision the versatility of the fabric more clearly.

With a nod of understanding, the salesman quickly disappeared into the vastness of the factory. As I awaited his return, I took the opportunity to explore the other fabrics on display. Each texture, pattern, and colour had its own unique charm, but my heart remained fixed on the elegance and grace of pure silk.

As I touched and felt the different fabrics, evaluating their quality and drape, I couldn't help but anticipate the future of my clothing line. It was not just about creating garments, but about creating an experience. The fabric needed to be more than just a material; it had to be a conduit of sophistication and refinement.

After what felt like an eternity, the salesman returned with a collection of pure silk fabrics in both white and cream as I had requested. He carefully laid them out on the table, allowing the light to dance upon their smooth surfaces. The sheen of the silk caught my eye, shimmering effortlessly as if commanding attention. It was a sight to behold.

With every stroke of my hand, the silky texture whispered whispers of luxury and opulence. I could imagine the way it would caress the skin, effortlessly draping over the body, highlighting its beauty. The pure silk radiated an air of elegance that was hard to resist. As I examined each sample in detail, I knew that these fabrics were the perfect canvas for my vision.

They possessed all the qualities I had hoped for - delicacy, fluidity, and a touch of extravagance. In that moment, I could envision my clothing line coming to life, adorned by customers who appreciated the finer things in life.

Unable to contain my excitement, I signalled the salesman once more and inquired about the possibility of leaving with fifty meters of both fabric choices. As I explained my vision for these fabrics, the salesman listened intently and began to understand my passion. It was then that I proposed the idea of establishing a partnership, with the textile store becoming my brand's full-time supplier, offering discounted prices in return.

The thought of becoming partnered with the very place that had a stellar reputation, bringing luxury to my dream collection, was exhilarating. I knew that this partnership would not only benefit me but also the store, as it would become the prominent supplier for a brand close to hitting the city's red carpets.

With the fabrics in my possession, I left the store and hurried back home, eager to delve into the planning stage of my collection. Imagining the dresses in all their forms - draped, scooped, straight - filled me with a sense of wonderment. I visualized how each dress would accentuate the wearer's curves and exude an air of sophistication.

The white fabric, with its pristine purity, symbolized the epitome of gracefulness. It would be perfect for creating ethereal gowns, fit for a celebratory event, or for any special occasion where elegance was a must. The cream fabric, on the other hand, possessed a warmer tone, reminiscent of pure bliss.

It evoked images of romantic and vintage-inspired dresses, with delicate lace overlays and intricate embroideries.

As I meticulously planned the designs, I envisioned the overall vibe of my brand. I wanted it to be recognized for its attention to detail, its use of exquisite fabrics, and its commitment to providing women with dresses that made them feel confident and beautiful. The white and cream fabrics were the pillars upon which this vision would stand, elevating my collection to new heights.

Many hours were spent sketching, draping, and perfecting each design. The fabrics seemed to guide me as I let my imagination run wild, creating a collection that embodied the essence of elegance. The white fabric, so pure and delicate, lent itself effortlessly to flowing gowns, while the cream fabric added depth and richness to more structured silhouettes.

As the collection started to take shape, I realized that my vision was becoming a reality. The dresses that danced through my mind were now intricately woven into sketches and patterns. The symbiotic relationship between the fabrics and my designs was undeniable. They complemented each other, adding a touch of grandeur to the dresses' aesthetic.

My journey, from falling in love with those fabrics to planning my collection, had been a whirlwind of excitement and creativity. The partnership I had established with the textile store had proven to be invaluable, as the discounted prices allowed me to explore numerous design possibilities with the fabrics.

In today's world, fashion has become more than just a means of covering our bodies -

it has become a form of self-expression, a way of making a statement about who we are. As I stood in front of the mirror, scanning myself to assess the outfit I wore that day, I couldn't help but feel frustrated in a pair of trousers I wasn't one hundred percent satisfied with. Being someone with tall legs, finding good quality silk trousers long enough to touch the floor had always been a challenge.

The fashion industry has always been diverse, catering to various body types, styles, and preferences. However, it was apparent that there was a significant gap in the market for tall individuals like myself. It seemed like the fashion industry had overlooked the needs of those who desired well-fitted, high-quality clothes that made them feel confident and comfortable in their own skin.

Jeans, the go-to option for many, never quite suited my taste. My personal style had always leaned towards something more refined and elegant. I revelled in the poise and sophistication of fitted, good quality clothing that accentuated my figure and made me feel neat; but it seemed as though the fashion industry had forgotten about people like me, leaving us frustrated and disillusioned.

Filled with discontent, I made a decision that day - to take matters into my own hands and create multiple fashion statement that reflected my needs and desires. As one of my many clothing frustrations - I vowed to prioritize what had been consistently absent from the market - perfectly fitted, cream silk trousers that would gracefully drape down to the floor, embracing my long legs. Alongside it, a matching blazer, exuding power and confidence.
Fit for a boss.

Why should I settle for less when I knew exactly what I wanted and could make it happen?

It was time to challenge the fashion market that seemed to favour the average height individual. I sought to redefine the standards, to push boundaries, and to create a space where taller individuals could also find clothing that not only fit their bodies but also resonated with their personal style.

Fashion is not just about the clothes we wear; it is about how those clothes make us feel. It is about the power of self-expression and the ability to radiate confidence from within. By addressing the needs of individuals with different body types, my brand aimed to provide not just clothing, but a transformative experience, enabling people to embrace their individuality and unleash their true potential.

# BLUEPRINT

Social media has undoubtedly become a powerful platform where individuals and companies strive to project a positive image of themselves to the public. It has spawned a new digital world, where people carefully curate their online presence and companies strategically promote their products and services. This emphasis on presenting oneself or one's brand in a favourable light demonstrates the significant impact social media has on our society.

For individuals, social media serves as a means to gain popularity and approval from the general public. In this quest, individuals often focus on crafting a positive narrative through the content they share, whether it be words, photos, or videos. Every post is carefully constructed, ensuring that it aligns with societal norms and objectives. Individuals feel compelled to project an image that will resonate with others and secure their acceptance. This constant effort to put themselves in a positive light reflects the desire for validation and positive feedback from their online interactions.

Individuals with a professional agenda are highly conscious of their online reputation and are keen to avoid anything that might tarnish it.

The fear of negative judgments or the potential consequences of a poorly received post often leads individuals to filter and censor their content. In doing so, they meticulously curate their virtual persona, presenting themselves as a flawless version of their true selves. By focusing primarily on promoting the positive aspects of their lives, individuals aim to gain admiration and avoid potential criticism or social backlash.

In another breath, companies leverage social media as a tool to promote their products and services, but they go a step further by utilizing the platform for advertising. Companies recognize the potential of reaching a wide and diverse audience through social media platforms, influencing consumer behaviour, and boosting sales. With each post, tweet, or update, companies aim to captivate users' attention, endorsing their brand and products in the most enticing manner. Advertisements seamlessly integrate into users' feeds, blurring the distinction between content and promotion. This strategy encourages social media users to engage with these ads, increasing the likelihood of driving sales and revenue.

Many individuals and companies succumb to a culture of comparison and competition, ultimately leading to self-doubt and insecurity. The pressure to constantly present an idealized version of oneself or one's brand can be overwhelming and detrimental to mental well-being. While this emphasis on presenting a positive narrative may be beneficial in some respect, it is crucial to maintain a balance and not lose sight of the authenticity and genuine connections that make social media a powerful tool in our increasingly digitized world.

***

From a mere fifteen-hundred-page followers to twelve thousand on a particular social media platform for my brand's page, the pressure quickly mounted as I realized that I am the face of the brand. All posts had to be immaculate, indirectly screaming at my target audience to drop everything and purchase from the website. It was equally fun to monitor the page, scrolling through my followers' posts and comments about my products. It always seemed to grab a piece of my heart, seeing how many people valued me and my work.

The journey on the brand's social media platforms was a true reflection of direct or indirect advertisement. As the page's sole representative, I bear the responsibility of portraying the brand's essence and capturing the attention of potential customers. Every post I create becomes a window into the world of Aluel Deng, a magnet that urges the audience to explore further and make a purchase.

With the increasing number of followers, the stakes heightened. I could no longer afford to produce mediocre content or slack off. Each post had to be carefully crafted, ensuring its appeal to my target audience and radiate a compelling message. The pressure to create immaculate posts, capable of mesmerizing my followers and compelling them to act, consumed me. The responsibility was both thrilling and demanding, as I strived to depict my brand in a captivating light.

Amidst the demanding nature of the task at hand, there was an undeniable joy in monitoring my page's progress. Scrolling through my followers' posts and comments about the products became a daily ritual that never failed to bring a surge of pride.

Witnessing the genuine appreciation and value people placed on my creations never failed to touch my heart. It was a humbling experience to see the impact my work had on others, inspiring them to share their joy and satisfaction with the world.

No longer was my brand just a collection of products; it had evolved into a thriving community, bound together by their appreciation and loyalty towards my work. Their support became my motivation to go above and beyond, continually striving to deliver the best products and create remarkable content that would resonate with their desires.

With each comment and post, I became more invested in the growth and success of my brand. Their feedback, whether positive or constructive, provided valuable insights and highlighted areas where I could improve. My followers became my trusted companions on the journey, guiding me towards developing a brand that not only met their needs but also surpassed their expectations.

At times, the responsibility of being the face of the brand felt overwhelming. The weight of representation and by extension, myself, rested heavily on my shoulders. But the support and validation from my growing community never failed to push me forward, giving me the strength to persist and embrace the challenges head-on.

My personal social media page, however, held significant importance in my life. It had grown into a community of individuals who respected and admired me, not only due to the prominent status my family held, but mainly because of the personal and professional achievements I have accomplished overtime. With time, it was noticeable that there were also group of young women who were inspired by my story, my journey of overcoming challenges and -

emerging victorious with the undeniably strong drive to excel in the roles I undertook. The support received from these individuals was invaluable, wanting to always prioritize engagement with them whenever possible.

Throughout my life, I had been fortunate to have the support of family, who held notable positions in society. The reputation paved the way for connections and associations that helped shape my personal journey. While this may have been a basis for admiration, what truly matters to me is the effort I put into creating my own unique identity, independent of external privileges. It is the recognition of my personal accomplishments, fuelled by hard work and dedication, that brings significance to me as an individual.

Beyond the perceived glamour, my page served as a platform of inspiration for numerous young women. By sharing my story, the challenges I faced, and the resilience exhibited, the aim was to empower others to confront their obstacles head-on. The ability to connect with people on a personal level, providing them with the motivation to tread a similar path of triumph, is a responsibility I took seriously; consequently making it a point to engage with these individuals, offering words of encouragement and guidance whenever possible.

Engagement on social media is not a trivial matter; it is an opportunity to build meaningful connections and inspire others. These connections transcend the virtual realm and often translate into real-life relationships. For this reason, I invested time and effort into actively engaging with the community that had developed around my page. Be it offering advice, answering questions, or simply lending an empathetic ear to those who reached out - encouraging an environment of mutual support and growth.

The digital age has brought numerous possibilities, but it has also spawned a culture of superficiality and inauthenticity. By using my page to share both successes and failures, it was of personal importance to present an authentic portrayal of my life. It was important to me that the people who looked up to me recognized the whole picture—the highs as well as the lows. This transparency not only made me relatable but also allowed others to learn from my experiences and realize that failure is not synonymous with defeat.

\*\*\*

Scrolling through my phone one Sunday afternoon, I found myself clicking on a specific social media platform, eager to catch up on the latest updates from my friends and favourite pages. Little did I know that this brief moment would lead me to an intriguing encounter.

As the page loaded, my eyes were immediately drawn to a familiar sight – my own photos. A caption accompanied the pictures that read, "Aluel Dim Deng makes moves with her latest endeavour." Curiosity piqued; I could not resist delving into the details of what I had seemingly accomplished. However, upon closer inspection, I noticed it was not a personal post but rather shared by a trendy blog page.

Intrigued yet hesitant, I scanned the page to find out who had deemed my endeavour worthy of sharing. It was in that moment that I began to truly understand the power of social media. The virtual space serves as a platform for both positivity and hate, a space where stories are shared, and opinions collide. But it was the fear of encountering negative comments that made me question whether it was worth diving into the depths of this post.

Nevertheless, curiosity outweighed caution. I cautiously began to delve into the vast expanse of three-hundred comments that unfolded beneath the post. With each comment, I found myself enveloped in a dichotomy of emotions. Most comments emanated positivity, words of appreciation, eagerness to engage with my businesses, and support. It was heart-warming to witness strangers celebrating my achievements, proving that the virtual realm can foster genuine connections.

However, amidst the warmth of uplifting comments, there were the occasional bursts of negativity, seemingly fuelled by envy. These hate-filled remarks served as a sobering reminder of the darker side of social media. People often hide behind their screens, spewing vitriol under the guise of anonymity. It is in these moments that our vulnerability is exposed, and our resolve to ignore the negativity is tested.

Consciously aware of the inevitable presence of hateful comments, I had long ago established a rule for myself – to never read comments on blog pages related to me. This rule served as a shield against the potential harm that virtual words could temporarily inflict on my emotional well-being. After all, it is far too easy for individuals to type away their jealousy or resentment without any consequences.

In response to the post, I chose to react with a simple love heart, expressing my gratitude for the positive sentiments shared. And with that, I silenced my phone, retreating to my safe haven of aviation documentaries. It was in the tales of great adventurers and the marvels of aviation that I found solace from the tumultuous world of social media.

As I settled into my cosy armchair, ready to indulge in the riveting world of aviation through a captivating documentary, I couldn't have anticipated the incessant flashing of my phone that would disrupt the tranquillity of my evening. It appeared the world outside was desperate to invade my personal space, demanding an immediate response. It was undoubtedly a consequence of the latest blog post, as I assumed family and friends were eager to voice their thoughts and opinions.

Annoyed by the constant interruptions, I hastily contemplated putting my phone completely off, hoping to stop the incessant flashing. However, experience had proven that this was not an effective solution. Messages and notifications continued to infiltrate my peace; their unwelcome arrival felt like an invasion of privacy. Frustrated and in need of respite, I made a decision that would truly sever the connection between me and the virtual world for the next few hours.

Placing the device on a nearby table, I turned it upside down, deliberately ignoring every notification and message that dared to make itself seen. With an air of defiance, I distanced myself from the constant pull of virtual correspondence, yearning for a moment of undisturbed tranquillity.

As the aviation documentary unfolded before my eyes, I couldn't help but be swept away by the sheer fascination of the subject matter. The stories of brave pilots and the awe-inspiring beauty of the skies intertwined to create a symphony of passion and admiration within me. With every passing minute, my desire to experience the magic of flight first hand grew.

The very thought of soaring through the cerulean skies, drifting amidst cottony clouds, and embracing the cool caress of the wind filled me with a sense of profound longing. The imagery painted by the documentary transported me to distant lands, enticing me to embark on yet another adventure. There was an itch within me, urging me to break free from the mundane routine and immerse myself in unfamiliar territories, seeking the thrill that only travel could provide.

As the documentary neared its end, the yearning for a vacation became a resounding echo within my mind. The routine of daily life seemed a stark contrast to the excitement and wonder that awaited outside my comfort zone.

In this hyperconnected world, where virtual interactions often take precedence over tangible experiences, the aviation documentary stood as a reminder of the beauty found in exploration and discovery. It encouraged me to break free from the shackles of the digital realm and set sail towards the unknown, where the thrill of the unexpected resides.

Although now my work phone begun to flash, reminding me of the virtual reality I had momentarily abandoned, I found solace in the thought that there was a pending adventure waiting to be embraced. It was time to trade swiping for wandering, emojis for genuine smiles, and online conversations for heartfelt conversations with both new and familiar faces.

I craved the adventure of wandering through ancient ruins, the elation of standing atop majestic mountains, the tranquillity of exploring serene beaches, and the -

immersion into different cultures. I yearned to taste exotic cuisines, to listen to unfamiliar melodies, and to witness customs and traditions that had thrived through generations.

It was then that I realized how much I had allowed myself to be consumed by the allure of virtual correspondence, missing out on the richness of the real world that awaited me. The world was out there, beckoning me to embrace its endless possibilities, its diversity, and its beauty. I owed it to myself to break free from the confines of my device and rather at its side, to immerse myself in a world that could never be reached through a screen.

\*\*\*

Dubai, the land of opulence and grandeur, has always intrigued me with its towering skyscrapers, luxurious hotels, and vibrant culture. As I once again flew out of London Gatwick Airport and set foot on the Dubai soil, a wave of nostalgia washed over me. The familiar scent of Oudh wafting through the air before the arrivals area immediately transported me back to the vivid memories of Regal.

After taking care of the necessary administrative tasks, such as registering a local sim-card, I found myself navigating through the sizeable airport. The sheer enormity of Dubai International Airport never ceased to astound me. As I wandered through the bustling crowds, I marvelled at the fusion of nationalities converging here, each person contributing to the diverse tapestry that is Dubai.

Finding the exit seemed like a daunting task amidst the chaotic bustle of the airport. Nevertheless, my determination to embrace the city's allure pushed me forward. With my eyes scanning the surroundings, I finally located the exit, where a fleet of taxis awaited their eager passengers. The sight of those vehicles marked the beginning of my adventure in this mesmerizing city.

I had made a rather foolish decision to visit Dubai during the hottest month of the year. As I walked towards the taxi stand, I could feel the scorching heat embracing me with its relentless intensity. Temperatures rose to a sweltering high of mid-forty degrees at night, leaving no room for relief or respite. The desert heat overwhelmed the environment, casting a blistering glow to the naked eye - which in actuality, was sweat.

Climbing into the air-conditioned cocoon of the taxi, I prayed for a temporary escape from the sweltering heat outside. As the car zoomed across the highways, I observed the striking contrasts of Dubai's landscape. The sleek modernity of the city's architecture juxtaposed against the ancient Arabian sand dunes that lay beyond its periphery. This harmonious blend of tradition and progress was a testament to Dubai's ongoing transformation into a global hub.

Leaning back in the plush seat, I reflected on the marvels this city holds. From the iconic Burj Khalifa piercing the clouds to the man-made archipelago of Palm Jumeirah, Dubai is a testament to mankind's ability to conquer and create. But it was not just the grandeur of its structures that captivated me. It was the hospitality of its people, the fusion of cultures, and the tireless pursuit of excellence that left an indelible mark on my heart.

As I made my way to the hotel, I was overwhelmed by a excitement and anticipation. I knew that Dubai would once again immerse me in a world of luxury and extravagance. But beyond its materialistic façade, I knew that this city had a soul – a vibrant energy that pulsated through its streets and enthralled all those who dared to explore it.

London Gatwick Airport may have been thousands of miles away, but the familiar scent of Oudh constantly lingered in my senses, connecting me to the familiarity of Dubai. As the taxi approached the hotel, a smile crept upon my lips. I was ready to embark on a new adventure, to unravel the mysteries of this extraordinary city, and to let its charm intoxicate me.

Days after settling in, situated in the heart of the UAE, I finally got into a productive routine.

Dubai, a bustling city, proved to be more than just a place to holiday, it was a haven brimming with opportunities for entrepreneurs. Whether one was a noviceventuring into the world of business or an experienced individual on behalf of their company, looking to expand their ventures, it provided an environment where success seemed attainable. The city's electric atmosphere was permeated with an aura of motivation, inspiring and igniting the entrepreneurial spirit within its inhabitants.

The rapidly growing economy and an infrastructure that rivals some of the most developed cities in the world, offered a welcoming environment for entrepreneurs and professionals alike. The government's unwavering commitment to fostering a business-friendly ecosystem was evident in the various initiatives and policies established to support start-ups and small businesses. From an extensive network of free zones offering tax benefits and simplified regulations to access to funding and mentorship programs, Dubai seemed to have created the perfect breeding ground for entrepreneurial success.

The air itself seemed to be infused with motivation, as if an invisible force propelled individuals to pursue their dreams and make a mark in the business world. The drive and ambition of the people were infectious, creating an environment where collaboration and innovation thrived.

Walking through the streets of Dubai, one could not help but notice the vibrant start-up scene. Co-working spaces were filled with individuals brainstorming, networking, and exchanging ideas. The city was a melting pot of cultures, attracting entrepreneurs from all corners of the globe.

This diverse mix of talents and perspectives fostered an atmosphere of creativity, where innovative solutions to societal problems emerged from the collaborative efforts of individuals with different backgrounds and experiences. Its strategic location at the crossroads of Europe, Asia, and Africa made it a hub for international trade and investment. The city's excellent connectivity and world-class infrastructure facilitated business expansion, attracting multinational corporations looking to establish a regional presence. The abundance of business conferences, expos, and networking events further catalysed growth and provided opportunities for budding entrepreneurs to showcase their ideas and forge valuable connections.

As I immersed myself in the entrepreneurial culture of Dubai, I could not help but feel optimistic, absorbing the scene that proved to have limitless possibilities. The city's energy was contagious, inspiring everyone to dream larger. It seemed apparant that people were encouraged to take risks, learn from mistakes, and embrace the entrepreneurial journey without judgement.

Taking the opportunity to fully relax in a prestigious city and do things that I wouldn't usually do in the UK, I decided to book a full pamper day for myself; but instead of going to a spa or salon, I had the idea of bringing the pampering experience to me by having a team of professionals come to my residence. Little did I know that this decision would lead to an unforgettable experience.

Excitement filled the air as I eagerly awaited the arrival of the pamper team. I had been working tirelessly for months, and this day of relaxation was much needed. When the doorbell finally rang, I hurriedly made my way to the front door.

As I opened it, I was greeted by four lovely ladies from a nearby beauty salon. They were adorned in white uniforms, carrying sophisticated equipment carefully packed into their bags. Their warm smiles instantly made me feel at ease.

As the professionals settled in, arranging their desks and equipment, I quickly realized that this pampering day was going to be a treat for all my senses. I rushed into the kitchen, intent on preparing some tea and snacks for my new guests. I wanted them to feel just as pampered as I did. It was important to me that this experience was enjoyable for both parties involved.

As I re-entered the room, the scent of aromatic oils filled my nostrils, immediately transporting me to a state of tranquillity to add to the pretence of being in an actual spa. My guests sat in their designated spots, ready to completely transform me.

In between sips of tea and bites of snacks, we engaged in lively conversations that made the entire experience feel like a gathering of close friends. We discussed various topics, ranging from travel adventures to personal anecdotes. It felt like a breath of fresh air, as I had been so consumed by the busyness of everyday life that I rarely had the chance to unwind and truly connect with others.

Throughout the pampering session, I allowed myself to fully immerse in the experience. The professionals skilfully worked their magic, providing a range of treatments that left me feeling rejuvenated and renewed. From a manicure and pedicure to a facial and massage, each moment was a sensory delight. The foot massage, in particular, proved to be the pinnacle of relaxation, and I found myself struggling to keep my eyes open.

As the beauty therapy ended, I couldn't help but feel a longing for a longer session of pure bliss and relaxation. Not only had I thoroughly enjoyed a day of pampering, but I had also forged connections with these four incredible women who had dedicated their time to make me feel special. Their genuine care and expertise had truly transformed the atmosphere, turning a simple appointment into an unforgettable experience.

\*\*\*

A few mornings later, as I woke up, I began to feel the effects of boredom. The initial excitement that accompanied the anticipation of this relaxing holiday had faded away, leaving me with an overwhelming restlessness. It seemed that the idleness was starting to take its toll on me, and I desperately needed something to occupy my mind.

As I sat on the balcony, sipping my morning coffee, I started to brainstorm ideas that could help me overcome this dull state of mind. Suddenly, a thought struck me – why not use this time to put the perfume oils I had planned some time back into fruition? After all, my passion for creating fragrances had been an integral part of my life within the last two years, and I was in the perfect location to make all of this possible, especially in a short period of time.

Reflecting on my hit perfume, Regal, I realized that there was room for improvement. The scent had gained popularity and a loyal customer base, but it lacked versatility. It was a traditional spray perfume that targeted a specific market, whereas people's preferences for fragrances varied greatly.

The idea excited me instantly. Oil-based perfumes had become quite popular in recent years, known for their longer-lasting scent and ability to interact with the wearer's body chemistry in a unique way. But I wanted to take it a step further and create a range of options with different fragrant notes to cater to different noses, especially considering the survey I had conducted whilst in South Sudan a few weeks prior.

Without wasting any more time, I grabbed my notepad and started jotting down the possible variations of the scent, that I could create as oil-based perfumes. I tweaked the original fragrance slightly to enhance its characteristics and make it even more delightful. The possibilities were endless – a lighter and fresher version for those who preferred a subtle scent, a more floral option for those with a romantic taste, a woody variant for those who loved earthy fragrances, and a citrus-based oil for those seeking a vibrant and refreshing aroma.

Not only would this decision provide an exciting new experience for my customers, but it would also allow them to choose a scent that truly spoke to their individuality. It was a win-win situation – my business would benefit from increased sales, and my customers would find satisfaction in having a product tailored to their preferences.

A place where luxury and opulence reign supreme, the city's desire for exceptional customer service seemed to be the norm. As I embarked on my exploration of Dubai, I discovered that some stores took exclusivity to another level by implementing a system of appointments for tailor-based service and attention. Intrigued by this concept, I eagerly sought out such an establishment and was fortunate enough to secure a same-day appointment at a pure fragrant oil factory.

With great anticipation, I hailed a taxi and directed the driver to Bur Dubai, the location of the factory. The scorching heat welcomed me as I stepped out of the vehicle, but my excitement overshadowed any discomfort. Determined to experience the epitome of personalized service, I made my way into the factory building, prepared to be enchanted by the wonders within.

Entering the building, I found myself in a small but elegant elevator. The air conditioning provided immediate relief from the outdoor heat, and I savoured the refreshing coolness that enveloped me. As the elevator glided smoothly to the desired floor, I couldn't help but feel a sense of exclusivity and anticipation. This unique mode of entry only solidified my belief that this experience would be unlike any other.

As the elevator doors opened, I was greeted by an air of tranquillity that contrasted with the bustling city outside. The hum of machinery in the background filled the air, creating a harmonious symphony, pleasantly reminding me of my office in Juba.

Being forced out of a daydream, a petite, neatly dressed lady appeared before me, expressing genuine hospitality. Her welcoming smile made me feel instantly at ease, as if we were old friends reuniting.

With grace and expertise, and after a brief seated discussion, she guided me through the factory, showcasing the meticulous process behind the creation of each fragrant oil. We passed rows of sleek stainless-steel containers and vats, where the transformation from raw materials to exquisite scents took place. The fragrant oils, meticulously bottled and packaged, gleamed with pride.

As we walked and talked, the lady passionately shared stories about the traditions and history of perfumery in the United Arab Emirates. She explained how each fragrance was carefully crafted to embody the essence of the region, allowing visitors to take a piece of Dubai's enchantment with them. The amount of care and attention to detail invested in each fragrance was truly remarkable. It was evident that this factory was more than just a production facility; it was a haven for perfume enthusiasts, a place where craftsmanship and artistry converged.

Inspired by the beauty and craftsmanship I had witnessed, I decided to initiate a partnership with the factory, just as I had done a few weeks prior with the fabric factory. With Salma's guidance, we made our way back to her office on the sixth floor, where I was given a form to fill out and sign. Despite the boring administrative tasks that took what felt like hours to go through, I was determined to make this partnership a success, to start when I'm back on UK soil.

But it wasn't just about the paperwork. As we wrapped up our meeting, I couldn't help but express my love for some of the scents I had encountered during the factory tour. Salma, with her generous spirit, happily offered me bigger sample sizes of the scents I had fallen in love with. It was a gesture that showcased not only her kindness but also the company's commitment to customer satisfaction.

As I left the factory, my bag filled with sample bottles of fragrant oils, I felt a wavering possibility. The partnership with this factory held immense potential for the expansion of my brand. By offering these unique, high-quality fragrances, I would not only be providing customers with a piece of Dubai's enchantment but also creating a new stream of revenue for the company.

Quickly making my way back home, I could feel the exhaustion setting in after enduring the scorching heat outside. Seeking solace, I immediately headed for the shower, desperate to relieve my body from the sickly heat that had engulfed me. As the refreshing water cascaded over me, the tension in my muscles began to dissipate, and a sense of calm washed over my weary soul.

Once rejuvenated, I decided to appease my hunger by preparing a simple yet delicious late lunch. The tantalizing aroma of pasta filled the air as it cooked to perfection, guaranteeing a much-needed break from the demands of the day. Accompanying the meal was a tall, cold glass of Coca Cola, the effervescence of which promised to quench my thirst and bring delight to my taste buds.

As I indulged in my meal, my thoughts wandered to the bag of goodies that Salma had generously bestowed upon me earlier. Little did I know, it held an unexpected surprise. Opening it with curiosity, I was shocked to discover not only the collection of fragrance oil samples, but also a handful of scent testing strips and ten miniature-sized bottles, specially designed to mix different oils together.

Overwhelmed by Salma's thoughtfulness and the level of customer service she had shown, it was imperative for me to express my gratitude. Swiftly, I composed a heartfelt message, outlining my immense appreciation for her kind gesture and the generosity she had displayed. It was a small act of reciprocation.

With my hunger satiated and my gratitude conveyed, I felt an eagerness to start the process early. Inspired by the tantalizing array of fragrance oils that lay before me, I decided to dive headfirst into the world of scent creation.

Preparing myself as if I were a chemist in a laboratory, I tied up my hair in a practical bun and adorned my hands with vinyl gloves, ready to embark on this familiar journey.

The process of creating my perfect scent was not something to be rushed; it required meticulous attention to detail and patience. Each time I combined different oils together, I carefully noted the proportions and observed the resulting patterns of fragrance. Day after day, I immersed myself in this sensory experiment, adjusting and refining my combinations, determined to achieve an impeccable blend that resonated with my individuality.

Five days elapsed; each day seeped in anticipation. Time seemed to pass both quickly and slowly, suspended in the realm of my fragrant creation. Although the journey was arduous, with moments of self-doubt and uncertainty, I was driven by an unwavering desire for perfection. The entirety of this sensory process became a labour of love, a testament to my dedication and the profound impact fragrance had on my life.

Finally, the day arrived when I stood before a blend that captured the essence of my being, the culmination of countless experiments and unwavering determination. It was as if I had discovered a masterpiece that perfectly mirrored my heart, soul, and dreams. The satisfaction that surged within me was immeasurable, validating the journey I had embarked upon.

Creating scents is an art form that requires precision, creativity, and an understanding of people's desires. As a perfumer, I took great pleasure in experimenting with fragrances, blending different notes and creating unique scents that would captivate my customers' senses.

Within that first scent creation, I decided to extend the range by offering three other variations, each tweaked slightly to cater to different preferences. I wanted to provide my customers with options and allow them to choose the scent that resonated with their individual desires. The first was stronger with a levelled array of sweet, but woody Oudh, giving it a luxurious and alluring appeal. This version was for those who wanted to make a bold statement and exude confidence with their fragrance.

The second variation was a diluted version of the original. While still carrying the essence of the authentic scent, it offered a lighter and more subtle aroma that gently tantalized the senses. This option was perfect for those who preferred a more understated fragrance, one that whispered enchantment rather than shouted it.

The third variation was a floral interpretation. I was inspired by the idea of incorporating the delicate and feminine allure of flowers into this deep and woody scent. The floral notes added a touch of elegance and evoked feelings of romance and grace. This version was intended to appeal to those who desired a softer and more feminine fragrance experience.

Finally, I introduced a cocoa-induced scent, a unique and unexpected combination that married the richness of chocolate with the earthiness of wood. The result was a scent that was warm, comforting, and indulgent. This variation was designed for those who wished to embrace their sensual side, enveloping themselves in a fragrance that evoked moments of pure bliss and relaxation.

With my creations complete, I meticulously went through my notepad, reviewing the calculations and ensuring that each ingredient was calculated precisely.

Perfumery is an intricate science, and every detail must be meticulously considered to achieve the desired experience. Checking and rechecking my calculations gave me the assurance that my creations were perfectly balanced and would bring joy to those who chose to wear them.

Many weeks had passed since the oils had settled into their airtight bottles. I had worn each of them, one at a time, day by day, carefully taking note of their lasting time on both my skin and clothes separately. I was determined to test them before getting into the hands of my customer base, subtly enticing those around me with alluring aromas, leaving a lasting impression. I also kept track of the number of times I was complimented on each fragrance, eager to discover which scent was praised the most. This extensive survey was a testament to the lengths I had gone through to ensure the success of this venture.

Weeks turned into months as I patiently awaited the results of my experiment. Compliment after compliment, it was clear that my efforts had paid off. The scents in the bottles had proven to be a resounding hit. People couldn't help but inquire about the captivating aroma that surrounded me. The positive feedback I received was encouraging, reinforcing my belief that I had stumbled upon something special.

Countless more visits to the factory were made, each time ensuring that I received the best of the best. The process of creating these perfume oils required attention to detail, creativity, and most importantly, a deep understanding of what the consumers desired. Salma was relentless in her pursuit of perfection of behalf of the company she was working for. She understood that success hinged on delivering a product that embodied luxury and elegance.

Finally, the launch day arrived. With the media's attention captured within minutes of the unveiling, it became clear that Aluel Deng's perfume oils had struck a chord with the public. Sales came flocking in, exceeding even my wildest expectations. The excitement and buzz surrounding these fragrances was palpable.

What set these perfume oils apart was their ability to evoke emotions and create a unique sensory experience. Each scent had been carefully crafted, using a combination of top-quality ingredients and expert knowledge. From the moment it touched the skin, the fragrance would unfold, revealing layers of complexity and sophistication. This meticulous attention to detail set Aluel Deng's perfume oils apart from the rest, ensuring immediate success.

***

After the successful launch of the brand's perfume oils, I knew it was time to quickly move onto the next product and capitalize on my love for silk, by introducing a new line of fashionable accessories to the market.

Scarves, traditionally associated with chilly weather conditions, were more than just a practical clothing item; they had the potential to serve as fashion statements. Recognizing this opportunity, I embarked on a journey to, again, find the perfect textile factory that would help me bring my vision to life.

Al Barsha, located in west Dubai, became the home of the hidden, ideal factory that aligned with my desires. It housed a team of highly skilled workers who were passionate about their craft and dedicated to ensuring that every detail, from the quality of silk to the intricate patterns on the scarves, met the highest standards.

The scarves, which I proudly named Monrovia, became a canvas for self-expression and style. They exuded elegance, sophistication, and a touch of uniqueness that resonated with fashion-forward individuals. With their rich colours and intricate designs, the Monrovia scarves became an instant hit among both the media and customers alike.

The success of the scarf line came as no surprise. In a region known for its love for fashion and luxury, the demand for high-quality accessories was ever-growing. The media attention garnered by my previous launch of the perfume oils further fuelled the interest in my brand's new venture, creating a buzz that attracted potential customers from all walks of life.

The Monrovia scarves, adorned with the distinctive 'Aluel Deng' logo, became a symbol of elegance and refinement. The attention to detail and the premium quality of the silk used in their production set them apart from other scarves available in the market. Each piece was a work of art, intricately crafted to ensure that my vision of creating timeless fashion statements was realized.

My time spent back and forth in Dubai had been nothing short of transformational. Initially, I viewed it as an opportunity to explore a new city and indulge in the luxuries it had to offer. However, little did I know that this land of wealth in abundance would prove to be more than just a vacation spot; it would become the catalyst for my career's success.

As I started to immerse myself in the Dubai lifestyle, I quickly realized the immense potential and opportunities that lay within its vibrant entrepreneurial ecosystem.

The city was bursting with innovation, attracting multinational companies and start-ups from around the globe. I began to view Dubai as the perfect breeding ground for my ideas to flourish.

Driven by this realization, I dedicated myself to leveraging this environment to propel my brand forward. With each visit, I meticulously worked on building my network and seeking collaborations with like-minded individuals. These efforts were not in vain. As I established valuable connections, my brand started to gain some recognition and credibility.

One milestone in particular that illustrated the progress I had made was when I received the coveted 'blue tick' verification on a social media platform. This verification, which signifies authenticity and influence, was a testament to the success and growth my brand had achieved. It opened doors to new opportunities, expanded my reach, and solidified my presence in the competitive world of social media branding.

The environment I placed myself in provided an unmatched platform for growth, not only through the influence of success stories surrounding me, but also its unparalleled emphasis on innovation and forward-thinking. The city enabled me to transform my ideas into profitable ventures. Had I just treated it like a vacation, I would have missed out on the incredible opportunities that presented themselves. By fully immersing myself in my heart's desires, I was able to expand on a thriving brand and establish myself as an influential figure in my field.

\*\*\*

The exhilarating feeling of lift-off and the realization that I was leaving behind the familiar streets of Dubai filled me with bittersweet sadness.

I had spent weeks in the bustling city, working tirelessly to achieve my goals and make significant progress in my work. As the plane ascended, I leaned my head back into the headrest, allowing a rare moment of rest to engulf me.

Touching down at London Gatwick Airport in the early hours of the morning, I was filled with a mix of suspense and uncertainty. It was a fresh start, a new chapter in my story, but also a reminder that there was still so much more to be done. The next day, week, and month held untold possibilities, and I knew that I couldn't afford to rest on my laurels.

My progressiveness over the years had become a driving force in my life, and it was this hunger that pushed me to constantly strive for more. I was acutely aware that the pursuit of great achievements often meant stepping into the unknown, taking risks, and embracing challenges. It was this mindset that had brought me to where I was, and it was this mindset that would propel me forward in the days to come.

As the plane taxied to its final stop, I swapped my sim card's, turned on my phone and was greeted by the constant pinging of messages and missed calls that had been left in my absence.

So, as I disembarked from the plane, armed with my experiences from Dubai and fuelled by my relentless drive, I felt a renewed sense of purpose. I was ready to conquer whatever lay ahead, fully aware that there were still countless goals to be accomplished, dreams to be fulfilled, and success to be attained.

In that moment, I smiled, knowing that my journey was far from over. With a heart filled with gratitude, I took more steps into the unknown, ready to push myself further and make the most of every opportunity that awaited me.

The true power lies in recognizing the impact we can have on others. From a simple smile to a profound conversation, our actions can touch the lives of individuals in ways we may never comprehend. As I think about the connections I have made and the lives I have touched, I can't help but feel excitement for what the future holds for them. Each person I have influenced adds their unique perspective and passions to the tapestry of life, creating a collective potential that is boundless.

The future is a canvas awaiting our individual and collective strokes. It holds the promise of growth, discovery, and endless possibilities. As I eagerly await the unfolding of my own journey, I am equally excited to witness the blossoming of those whose lives I have touched. Together, we have the power to create a world that is enriched with love, compassion, and understanding.

# REFLECTION

As the years unfurled and transformed from the tumultuous 2016, to the transformative 2023, my life embarked on a remarkable journey, evolving and embracing definitive characteristics. From the depths of frustration and fury to the heights of wholesome bliss, my experiences sculpted me into the person I am today. Looking back, it is clear that had I not heeded the call of curiosity in 2016, my trajectory would have been vastly different, devoid of the achievements and revelations that have shaped my existence.

Curiosity, an endlessly persistent force within me, tugged at my heart and implored me to explore the world beyond what was readily available. It whispered in my ear, beckoning me to step out of my comfort zone, to challenge the mundane and embrace the unknown. Had I ignored this gentle yet unwavering voice, my life would have remained stagnant, devoid of growth and change.

Listening to my curiosity in 2016 was the first step towards unravelling the enigma of my purpose and finding clarity in the direction I needed to take.

It was a transformative year that led me to self-discovery and uncharted territories of knowledge. While initially daunting, this journey brought forth countless opportunities for growth, enabling me to flourish and find my true passions.

Throughout the subsequent years, a myriad of variables influenced and guided me towards the path I was destined to tread. These variables acted as the compass that navigated me through the storms of uncertainty. They included mentors who illuminated my way, challenges that tested my resilience, and experiences that broadened my horizons.

Mentors played a pivotal role in shaping my understanding and direction. Their wisdom and guidance fostered profound growth within me, helping me uncover latent talents and untapped potential. These remarkable individuals were beacons of knowledge, offering insights and perspectives that I could never have acquired on my own. Through their mentorship, I gained confidence in my abilities and learned to approach each endeavour with determination and enthusiasm.

Challenges, though arduous and formidable, acted as catalysts for growth. They were the crucibles in which my true character was forged. Each obstacle I encountered provided an opportunity to learn, adapt, and evolve.

Initially, frustration and fury would consume me, but as I developed resilience and perseverance, these challenges transformed into stepping stones towards inner fulfilment.

Overcoming them not only bolstered my determination but also fortified my belief in the power of endurance and tenacity.

Travel and exposure have long been recognized as key components in personal growth and development. There is a certain inexplicable power in venturing beyond the familiarity of one's own city and immersing oneself in unknown territories. Personally, I have experienced the transformative effect that travel and exposure can have on one's life, as it pushed me to strive for improvement and gain a heightened perspective on the world around me.

When we leave behind the comforts and routines of our daily lives, we are thrust into an unknown environment that forces us to adapt and navigate new situations. It is in this state of unfamiliarity that we are often confronted with our true selves, our strengths, and our weaknesses. Like a subconscious trigger, the knowledge that we must either do better or sink begins to permeate our thoughts.

As we venture into different cultures and societies, we are exposed to diverse ways of thinking, living, and existing. We witness first-hand the vast range of possibilities in life and realize that our own perspectives are just a small part of a much larger tapestry. This realization broadens our horizons and allows us to break free from the limitations of our preconceived notions and biases.

We are no longer bound by the constraints of our own culture, but instead, we are free to adopt different perspectives, values, and ways of living. This openness to new ideas and experiences allows us to break free from tunnel vision that often accompanies our daily lives, and instead, embrace the boundless possibilities that the world has to offer.

In this state of unfamiliarity, where everything is new and unknown, we are given the opportunity to rediscover ourselves and redefine our identities. We are forced to confront our fears, limitations, and weaknesses, but we also discover hidden strengths, resilience, and adaptability that we may not have realized we possessed. This self-discovery is a gift that can only be obtained by stepping outside of our comfort zones and embracing the unknown.

Adding to this, meeting people from different walks of life provides a profound understanding of the disparities that exist within our world. We gain insight into the struggles, triumphs, and challenges faced by individuals who may come from significantly different backgrounds than our own. These encounters foster empathy and compassion, as we learn to appreciate and respect the unique journeys and experiences of others. The exposure to different cultures, customs, and beliefs creates a tapestry of knowledge and understanding that ultimately makes us better-rounded individuals.

Whether it's navigating language barriers, adapting to unfamiliar environments, or encountering unforeseen challenges, each experience chips away at our preconceived limitations and helps us realize our true potential.

These experiences exposed me to diverse perspectives, cultures and ideas, expanding my understanding of the world and my place within it. They taught me that life, with all its intricacies, was meant to be lived fully and passionately.
Still, as I reflect upon the transformation that occurred from 2016 to 2023, I remain grateful for the curiosity that ignited my journey.

It was this deep-seated desire to explore, learn, and grow that pushed me towards the path I was destined to tread. The variables that played a role in shaping my trajectory were invaluable in providing guidance, inspiration, and resilience. Each one worked in harmony to uncover my true potential, enabling me to achieve fulfilment and bliss.

As I embark on the next chapter of my life, I carry with me the lessons learned, the wisdom imparted, and the indomitable curiosity that sparked this remarkable metamorphosis. If I could leave you with one piece of advice from this, it would be to never doubt your capabilities. Throughout life, there will be moments when you question your abilities, when you wonder if you have what it takes to achieve your dreams. But I implore you to keep pushing forward, to keep believing in yourself even when doubt creeps in.

In this vast world we live in, most things are obtainable, if only we have the strength and determination to reach for them. We can achieve far more than we often give ourselves credit for. Our minds possess an incredible power, one that can be harnessed to push us to unknown heights, in order to fulfil our deepest desires.

Sometimes, life can become monotonous, routine, and it is easy to lose sight of our dreams in the midst of our everyday responsibilities. But even in the mundane, it is crucial to remember that your fight, your pursuit of your dreams, is a noble one. It is a fight that is worthy, a fight that will bring you growth, fulfilment, and happiness.

I can speak from personal experience when I say that, I too, once had a dream. It was a dream that started on a wintery day in 2016, amid grey skies and with a -

glimmer of hope in my heart. At that time, doubt swirled in my mind, clouding my belief in my own abilities. But I made achoice, a choice to never let doubt dictate my actions, a choice to embrace the unknown and pursue my dreams.

And let me tell you, that choice has made all the difference. It hasn't always been easy, there have been countless obstacles and moments of uncertainty. But with every hurdle I overcame, with every step forward I took, my belief in myself grew stronger. I discovered that I was capable of far more than I ever imagined.

Life is full of uncertainties, and it is inevitable that we will encounter curveballs and setbacks along our journey. These challenges have the potential to knock us off our feet and shake our confidence, but it is important to remember the strength and resilience that resides within us. We possess the power to overcome anything that comes our way.

When faced with adversity, it is crucial to tap into our inner reserves of perseverance. Often, it is during these difficult moments that we discover the depth of our own strength. We can endure hardships and rise above them, no matter how overwhelming they may seem. Setbacks can be disheartening and demotivating, making us question our abilities and losing faith in ourselves. However, it is in these moments that we must remind ourselves that failure is not the end. Instead, it is a valuable learning opportunity and a stepping stone towards future success.

Embracing failure allows us to grow, learn from our mistakes, and develop a greater understanding of -

ourselves and our capabilities.

To overcome challenges, it is crucial to adopt a mindset of sole resilience. Rather than seeing setbacks as setbacks, we should view them as opportunities for growth and personal development. This mindset shift allows us to approach difficulties with an open mind and a willingness to learn from them, rather than being defeated by them.

Taking risks is another essential aspect of overcoming challenges and reaching our full potential. Courageous individuals are not afraid to step out of their comfort zones and take calculated risks in pursuit of their goals.

By pushing ourselves beyond our limits, we unlock new levels of potential and discover hidden talents and strengths that we never knew we possessed. Believing in ourselves is equally important. Our self-belief shapes our actions, motivates us to keep going despite adversity, and gives us the confidence to pursue our dreams.

If we doubt our abilities and don't have faith in ourselves, we limit our own potential and hinder our success. It is crucial to cultivate a positive self-image and trust in our abilities, acknowledging that we can achieve whatever we set our minds to.

So, with that being said, here is my letter to you:


Dear friend,

As you set forth on your path, I wanted to take a moment to remind you of the power and potential that lies within you. Embrace the unknown that awaits you, for it is within the unexplored territories of life that we often find our greatest treasures.

You will encounter moments of frustration along the way, but do not let these deter you. Instead, let it serve as fuel to ignite the fire within you, propelling you to fight for your dreams.

My dear friend, for you possess a strength that knows no bounds. Break free from the chains of doubt and fear and embrace the limitless possibilities that lie ahead. Trust in your abilities, trust in your intuition, and trust in the path that you have chosen.

If no one has said it to you, I want you to understand the full extent of your hidden capabilities. Your talents, skills, and passions uniquely equip you for success. You possess within you a well of untapped potential, waiting to be unleashed.

Do not be afraid to take risks, to leap into the unknown, for it is in these moments of boldness that we often unearth our true capabilities.

While the road may be long and winding, remember that it is the journey itself that holds the most valuable lessons. Each experience, whether it be triumphant or challenging, moulds you into the person you were always meant to become.

Embrace the hardships, for they will strengthen your resolve. Celebrate the victories, for they will fuel your determination. Remember that growth comes not only from the destination but from the steps taken to reach it.

So, my dear friend, as you embark on this exciting adventure, do so with a sense of courage and conviction. Embrace the unknown, fight for your dreams, and above all, believe in yourself.

In closing, I want you to always remember these three words: You've got this. They may seem simple, but they hold within them a force of empowerment. Now go into the world and do what you do best, my dear friend.
Unleash the power within you.


With love and wholehearted belief,

Aluel D. Deng